MAIL ORDER

...STARTING UP, MAKING IT PAY

J. Frank Brumbaugh

MAIL ORDER
...STARTING UP,
MAKING IT PAY

CHILTON BOOK COMPANY
Radnor, Pennsylvania

Copyright © 1979 by J. Frank Brumbaugh
Published in Radnor, Pennsylvania 19089, by Chilton Book Company

Library of Congress Cataloging in Publication Data

Brumbaugh, J Frank.
　Mail order. . . starting up, making it pay.

Includes index.
　　1. Mail-order business—Handbooks, manuals, etc.
2. Self-employed.　I. Title.
HF5466.B813 1979　　　658.8′72　　　78-14623
ISBN 0-8019-6804-6
ISBN 0-8019-6805-4 pbk.

Designed by William E. Lickfield
Manufactured in the United States of America

15　16　17　18　　　8　7　6　5　4　3

For MARIAN WHITTINGTON MCLELAND,
*without whose encouragement and
assistance this book might never
have been written.*

Contents

MAIL ORDER
...STARTING UP,
MAKING IT PAY

Introduction to
Mail Order
Opportunity

Watching the giant companies becoming bigger and small businesses being absorbed or failing by the thousands every year might make you think the day of independent entrepreneur is long past, a part of the "good old days" which you will never see again. In many ways this is true. There is no longer a place for the little grocery store, the one-man tailor shop, the shoe-shine parlor, the neighborhood repairman, the one-man manufacturing business. In spite of the occasional successful specialty store, small-scale operations, whether in manufacturing, service, or sales, are fading from the American scene. They are usually undercapitalized, lack the necessary management skills, and are unable to take full advantage of trade discounts because of limited sales. Seldom can they meet the sales competition provided by large companies.

One field is still open to the entrepreneur, a field in which he is welcome and can prosper. Here the existence of large corporations actually works to the advantage of the small-scale operator, the one-man business starting on a shoestring. That field is mail order merchandising. Giant corporations like Sears Roebuck and Montgomery Ward have not only earned billions of dollars in mail order but their efforts have conditioned the public to buy by mail. The advertising profession has also helped. The public is receptive to mail order advertising and accustomed to making purchases by mail.

In mail order merchandising anyone with a wanted product or service can compete successfully with the biggest of commercial firms. Competition is seldom as rough as it appears at first glance. In fact, the mail order operator actually benefits from the proliferation of mail order companies and their advertising, while experiencing little competition from them or from local stores throughout the country. This is not only because the existence of other companies conditions the public to buy, but primarily because the *small* mail order operator usually does not sell the same items offered by the larger mail order companies or local stores. The small operator offers a product that is unique in some way—either the product or service itself is unavailable elsewhere, or the special way he offers an otherwise ordinary product or service makes it desirable.

No other business combines such a reserve of preconditioned and receptive customers with such minimal sales competition. No other field offers more opportunity to set up with such a small amount of capital or space. It takes very little money to launch a mail order business. It can be operated from the corner of a room, keeping overhead expenses to a minimum. Mail order is truly the field of golden opportunity and can provide a direct and easy road to a better income, self-sufficiency, even prosperity. *Anyone* (novice enterpreneurs, homemakers, retirees, and handicapped take note!) who has an idea, a few dollars, a corner in which to work, and the ambition to go into a successful business of his or her own can make a good living. You can expand both your business and your income by following closely the methods described in this book.

This book will give you all the information and instructions you will need to start and operate your own successful mail order operation. It will describe to you in plain words the psychology of the customer, the selection of a product or service, and the best ways to reach and interest potential customers at rock-bottom costs. It will show how to use classified ads to publicize your business and attract potential customers. It will reveal how to prepare low-cost advertisements that draw the maximum number of replies. It will tell you when you should continue to run the same advertisement month after month, when you should change format, how often you should advertise, and the best times to run your ads. It will demonstrate how to prepare and use leaflets, broadsides, and folders that turn interested inquirers into *buyers* of your product or service. It will explain how and when to turn to an advertising agency and your printer, and what to expect from each. It will detail how to choose paper and print and how to use pictures and cuts.

It will describe how to handle your mailing efficiently and inexpensively. It will discuss where to get mailing lists for direct mail sales and how to rent or sell your own lists. It will detail the equipment and supplies you need in your office and how to handle record-keeping and business expenses. It will show you how to handle customers, both the satisfied and the isolated few who aren't. It will tell you what you should know about money-back guarantees and how to handle returned merchandise. In short, it will tell you how to start your business and how to keep it running successfully.

Mail order is nearly foolproof, but it is not idiot-proof. You must guide your business with commonsense and know from month to month exactly how it is doing. You must keep your future customers aware of your product's availability by keeping your advertising campaign running smoothly. Though neither manual labor nor higher education is involved in operating your mail order business, it is no place for the lazy. Letters must be opened daily. Merchandise and advertising must be mailed. Bank deposits must be made, bills paid on time, and records must be kept up to date. Correspondence and order files must be maintained.

A mail order business will keep you busy, but it should not seem like work to you. If it does occasionally, think about the cash, the checks, the money orders which arrive in the mail each day, and the pleasure with which you deposit them in the bank.

1

You and Your Customers

Your decision to operate your own mail order business shows that you are ambitious and knowledgeable, that you recognize opportunity when it appears and want to turn it to your advantage. You know the immense profits to be earned in sales and you realize that *it is the owner of the business and not the employee who makes the most money*.

You also know that selling can be very hard work if *you* have to talk to each possible customer separately, but practically effortless if you make your advertisements do this hard work for you. You can talk personally to only a few people each day, whereas your ads give your message to thousands. You don't have to go out, find your customers, argue with them to make a sale. Your ads *force* customers to come to you and all your orders arrive in the mail. There is no personal contact.

Lack of personal contact is a great advantage. Each person is an individual and, if you were to meet that person face-to-face and try to make a sale, you would have to tailor your sales talk to that person alone. If you guessed right you would probably make a sale. If you guessed wrong, your time would be wasted and you would have made no money. The mail order customer, however, *when considered as a group* of thousands or millions of individuals, is much easier to analyze, to figure out, than is each individual person. Mail order customers are alike in more ways than you might think. And they are alike in ways which are not difficult to determine. *The ways in which people are alike are what you will use to plan your sales appeal*.

Scientists still do not agree on whether human beings have instincts as do lower animals. The important thing for you to remember is that *they act as if they have*. While the scientists argue you will use people's instincts and desires to make sales and increase your income. Our society causes each person to have desires he or she wants satisfied. People are no longer content, if they ever really were, with only the basic necessities of life—food, clothing, and shelter from the elements. They want more, much more. And they tend to want the same things. In fact, if you were to analyze the people of this country, or even the readers of a single newspaper, book, or magazine, according to their instincts, desires, likes, and dislikes, they would prove to be very much alike in many ways.

THE MAIL ORDER CUSTOMER: WHAT IS HE REALLY LIKE?

What are the instincts, characteristics, and desires that you need to know about people so you will know what to offer them and how to present it in the best way? Fortunately, market research by large advertisers has, over the years, accurately discovered what makes people tick. In the paragraphs which follow, all the major traits most people have in common are named and briefly discussed. These traits are possessed in varying degrees by 80 percent of *every* large group of people. This 80 percent is your customer. Because of the accuracy with which it has been analyzed, you can consider this immense group as one single individual. Thus, if you plan your sales appeal as if you were trying to sell to only this one person you will effectively reach most of your readers.

First, realize that your potential customer has money. He is willing to buy anything which he is convinced will be pleasurable to own. Price is important; so is quality. Properly combined in a unique or interesting product or service they make for instant acceptance.

Above all, your customer has had long experience with buying merchandise through the mails, and this experience has generally been satisfactory. Your customer is used to reading and acting on mail order advertising offers. He will read your advertisement *if you can catch his attention,* and, if you have done most of the right things and not too many of the wrong things, he is ready to pay your price in exchange for what you offer.

Your customer will tolerate delays of up to two or three weeks but shows signs of unrest if he has to wait much longer to receive his order.

He is not too receptive to advertising which attempts to sell merchandise direct. Although he is willing to gamble $2, $3, even $5 and often will buy sight unseen from ads at these prices, he is much more likely to reply to advertising which offers something absolutely free, even if what is offered is merely additional advertising and sales material. Rarely will he gamble sight unseen for amounts much greater than a couple of dollars, and higher priced items are rarely sold directly from the published ad.

Your customer is also less receptive to advertising which requires him to enclose a stamp or coin for postage or handling. Requested enclosures require the customer to write a letter and use an envelope. This he is often reluctant to do.

In fact, your customer hates to write letters, even to order something he really wants. So the easier you make it for your customer to reply to your offer, the more replies you will receive and the more sales you will make. If your initial ads *specify* or *suggest* that he can send a postcard and will receive information "absolutely free," you will get more returns and can place extensive advertising in his hands at low cost, advertising which *is* designed to produce an order and bring you cash.

Your average customer has unreadable handwriting. If you can get him to print his name and address you will save much effort and some unnecessary expense.

Your customer hates tiny coupons with lines too close together and too short for him to legibly fill in his name and address. Large coupons mean large ads. These, in turn, mean large expenses for you. They are unnecessary. Since you will usually do best with small ads, as explained in chapter 5, forget about coupons.

Your customer likes words and phrases such as *free, bonus, premium, guaranteed, your money back if unsatisfied, only one to a customer, pre-publication price, buy now before prices rise next month, orders shipped in 24 hours, sale, closeout prices, price reduced, reduced to 10 percent over cost, wholesale prices* and similar teasers. (There are hidden legal pitfalls in some of these phrases, and they should not be used indiscriminately. These terms are discussed in chapters 5 and 7.)

Your customer does not like to be made to think. Therefore, make all your ads and copy simple enough to be understood by a fourth-grade child. Your customer will not be insulted by simple language even if he holds graduate degrees. Rather, he will be pleased that he perceived your message without mental effort or concentration. Once mastered, this technique of getting your message across effortlessly actually makes many more people aware of your ad, even though they may not actually recall reading it with purpose. This is a legal and ethical form of subliminal advertising and is a major factor in increased response to your ads.

Your customer has developed habits in reading advertisements which you can cultivate to advantage. He often dismisses a full page display ad with a glance, yet will spend hours reading the fine print of classified ads. The classified ads have a strong attraction for the majority of people. They are often read for news and entertainment. Many times these casual readers will become your customers.

Your customer is suspicious of too-fancy advertising. Trickily designed mailing pieces and the lavish use of color, besides being very expensive, often have the opposite effect to that intended. Keep the wording clear and simple, and the material uncluttered.

He is also offended by high-pressure advertising. The soft sell is far more effective. It does not put the customer on the defensive. A defensive customer is hard to sell.

Your customer is usually suspicious. If you seem to offer much more than a legitimate bargain, he may reject your product or service. He knows no one can stay in business if he gives too much away, and he insists you prove your claims. Offer him an honest deal, and you have him at least half-sold.

Your customer is *mostly* honest. Very few of the checks you receive through the mail will bounce. But your customer also expects you to be honest—and if you expect to remain in business you must be! Honesty happens to be the most profitable policy as well.

Your customer is lazy. He rarely takes the trouble to return unsatisfactory purchases to mail order companies because it is too much trouble to repackage, rewrap, stamp the package, and take it to the post office. One little-known method of reducing merchandise returns is used by all the book, tape, and record clubs. *They design the shipping carton so it has to be destroyed to remove the contents*. Faced with a book, tape, or record he does not want and lacking a suitable shipping carton since the original is unusable, the chances are excellent that the book, tape, or record will not be returned. This occurs despite assurances that undesired merchandise may be returned for credit or "your money immediately refunded."

Your customer is thirsty for knowledge upon almost any subject. However, not wishing to think too much, he wants his knowledge predigested and in palatable doses. He doesn't want to study, although he will if the study can be made to seem pleasurable. Your customer will buy "how-to" books on any subject as long as your advertising convinces him he will need to expend little or no effort to master the subject. He also buys such books to read for pleasure, to escape into a dream, knowing full well he will never actually *do* the things espoused in the "how-to" book. This universal quirk of human nature provides many customers to mail order dealers in this type of product. The words "how-to" in the title sells many books which might otherwise never find buyers.

The book you are reading is a how-to book. Many of you will dream of becoming a mail order dealer with your own company and income, and *some* of you actually will. Others will enjoy dreaming about it but put this book on the shelf indefinitely. This book delivers what it says it will. It will teach you all you need to know to be successful in mail order. *Whether you use it to get ahead or merely dream about it, the choice is up to you.*

This is true of many products and services successfully offered through the mail. They appeal to the customer's personal desires and suggest that the simple purchase of your product or service will help satisfy those desires. And in fact it will.

Your average customer is frustrated. He is caught in a vicious circle of work—earn—spend—work. He thinks he would like to get out of the rat race if only he knew how. He yearns for the simpler, slower life of the "good old days." This is a basic urge traceable to primitive instincts and opens up a very large market for mail order dealers whose products cater to this universal dream. This aspect is discussed in detail in chapter 3.

Your customer really wants to be friends. He has a starry-eyed view of goodness in the world. A friendly approach will sell more goods than any amount of exhortation.

Your average customer. especially the housewife, is lonely and actually welcomes the arrival of direct mail as a friend. Such mail offers are read more often and more thoroughly than you might suspect.

Your customer is unsophisticated though he tries to appear very worldly and knowing. He is very receptive to a quiet, homey ad, simply worded, easy to read and to understand. Nevertheless, your customer has a "Walter Mitty" complex. He sees himself in heroic situations, grandly accepting praise. This makes the customer receptive to anything which makes him feel important, attractive, worldly, magnanimous, charitable, superior, loved, wanted, needed, or accepted. Keep this in mind when you choose your product or service and prepare your advertising.

Your customer is often superstitious but ashamed to admit it. A subtle approach to play upon his superstitions can bring sales but must be handled with extreme care. Your customer can be extremely touchy about his superstitions.

Your customer is interested in sex. Properly and smoothly handled, sex can add to sales. Use it honestly, however, and keep it clean or you may offend more than you interest.

Your customer also has a sense of humor. He appreciates clever humor but is seldom *sold* with such an approach. Use humor very carefully to establish rapport if you use it at all, but make your sales pitch in simple, straightforward language. Don't be too clever or you will lose a possible sale. In general, *all* puns should be avoided.

YOUR CUSTOMER'S GOALS AND VALUES

Because the customer *always* reads your ads with the question "What's in it for me?" uppermost in his mind, this is the question you must be sure to answer in your ads. The customer's selfish-appearing attitude is based upon his most basic instinct—self-preservation. *This is the number one instinct which makes people act as they do and it is the most important trait of all for you to remember.* The instinct for self-preservation is the basis of our interest in financial security and status, our concern for our families' security and well-being, our desire for self-esteem and earning the esteem of others, and many other concerns that make people potential purchasers of your product or service.

The "What's in it for me?" that your customer has in the back of his mind when he's reading your advertising can be any one or more of the following.

Better health—Your customer wants to feel or look better, live longer, have fewer illnesses. One cannot be happy without good health.

More money—Everyone wants more money. More money means that one can supply all one's needs and desires. This is a very potent motive. Even more important to the customer than *earning* money is *saving* it, getting more for less. A person will do much more to *keep* what he has than he will to add to it.

Popularity—Admiration by others, personal beauty, attractive personality, skills not possessed by everyone—all are of interest to the customer.

Comfort—Anything which gives comfort, ease, convenience, or luxury will be bought.

Leisure—The desire for leisure is basic. Most people do not really like to work; they would much rather do what they want to do when they want to. Cater to this real desire to travel, to play, to be without responsibilities.

Accomplishment—Every person takes pride in his accomplishments, in what he has made with his own hands, and in adding beauty or value through his own efforts.

Appearance—Personal appearance and that of home, car, and community is a source of pride.

Security—This is a powerful desire in most people. They desire independence, income, health, a reduction of risks, and time to enjoy life.

Praise—Everyone likes to be praised and admired, both for himself and his accomplishments and possessions.

Advancement—Every person wants recognition, a better job, a new title, to climb higher socially.

More fun—Ours is a leisure-oriented society. People play harder than they are willing to work and are always searching for fun, for new ways of pleasure.

Pride—Even the lowliest, most humble person has pride. This is a strong emotion, deeply seated in everyone.

Acquisitiveness—"Keeping up with the Joneses" is more than a cliché; it expresses man's basic nature to want and try to get everything he can for himself and his family. *Remember, one of the first words a baby learns is "Mine!"*

Creativity—Man is basically creative. Everyone believes he can paint or write "if only I had the time." He enjoys creating beauty as well as utility.

Efficiency—Because it is man's nature to be lazy he is always in the market for anything to make his job easier, to reduce the amount of work or thinking he must do.

Influence—"It isn't what you know, it's who you know that counts" is becoming truer every day. Everyone wants to have power over others, to influence or control what others do.

Curiosity—Progress results from man's curiosity. He is always interested in the new, the different, the unusual.

Self-Improvement—Most people are interested in improving their appearance, knowledge, or abilities—as long as it doesn't take much time or effort.

"In"—The herd instinct is almost as old as man. He wants to be recognized as one of the group, as "in" instead of "out." He also wants to be different—but only a little bit different.

WHAT YOUR CUSTOMER LOOKS FOR IN YOUR PRODUCT

Well, now you know what your customer is like and the kinds of goals and values he has. But what does he want to see *in your product*? What characteristics of a product or service will appeal to him?

Your customer will be favorably impressed by a product or service which:

Is fun to own, look at, or use
Is stylish or fashionable
Adds to his comfort
Gives him pleasure
Caters to his basic needs or desires
Offers pride of ownership
Eliminates some fear, real or imaginary
Proves his devotion to his family
Satisfies his curiosity
Is ornamental
Closely imitates something very expensive
Is well constructed with evident good workmanship
Expresses his loyalty to country, community, group, or family
Promotes companionship
Shows his devotion
Expresses his sympathy
Has beauty
Indicates his authority or social position

Proves he is ambitious
Gives him an advantage over rivals
Promotes harmony
Expresses his individuality
Has to do with travel
Causes envy in others

Your customer will be most receptive to an advertising appeal which indicates your product or service:

Is healthful
Promotes cleanliness
Is scientifically constructed
Saves time
Is appetizing
Is efficient
Is safe to own or use
Is durable, long-lasting, and will not break easily or wear out too soon
Is modern in every way
Appeals to his family
Supports his reputation or makes it better
Is fully guaranteed
Is medicinal
Is as attractive or useful as one more expensive
Appeals to his sense of elegance
Saves him money to buy or use
Is necessary or desirable to enjoyment of sports
Expresses his hospitality
Should be used instead of a substitute
Promotes a feeling of togetherness with others
Adds to his comfort
Is recommended by experts or authorities
Is socially superior
Is imported from exotic lands
Will add beauty to home, car, or surroundings

SUMMARY OF YOUR CUSTOMER'S TRAITS

Below is a summary of your customer's traits as described earlier in this chapter. Your customer has many of these characteristics, and they are the keys upon which you should base your choice of product or service and the way it is promoted in your advertising. Your customer:

Reads advertising
Often reads classified ads
Has money to spend
Will buy if you appeal to his needs and desires
Tolerates short delays
Is basically honest
Is acquisitive but not genuinely ambitious
Is somewhat lazy
Wants everything made easy for him
Wants knowledge served in easy doses
Dislikes having to think
Dislikes high-pressure or too-clever advertising
Is receptive to clear, simple, carefully chosen words
Responds to friendly approaches
Does not like to write letters
Hates tiny coupons and prefers not to tear them out of magazines
Is often a poor manager of time and money
Is always looking for bargains
Dislikes taking risks, but will gamble in small amounts
Desires security without effort or risk
Is frustrated by the pattern of modern life
Longs for the "good old days" or thinks he does
Is unsophisticated but unwilling to admit it
Is afraid of anything he does not understand
Is superstitious but unwilling to admit it
Is often suspicious
Can be surprisingly gullible at times
Often acts illogically
Likes to be the first to own something new
Has a sense of humor
Is interested in sex and receptive if handled smoothly
Has a secret Walter Mitty complex
Secretly feels he is superior to others and wonders why his obvious
 (to him) superiority is not recognized

PEOPLE CHANGE ONLY ON THE SURFACE

Values are not constant; they are always changing. Recent market research suggests that some values particularly relevant to people's spending patterns are gradually becoming different. These trends indicate: an increasing interest in quick material success; a tendency to spend money more readily; the desire to move about, to see new sights, to have new experiences; an increased willingness to indulge themselves; a greater acceptance of the new and unusual; a feeling that the world owes them a living and that the government should take care of their basic needs; a greater tendency to seek entertainment outside the home and family; an increased love of luxury and the desire for expensive things; a lowering of the standards of good taste; and increased dependence upon quick impressions and snap judgments.

This does not mean that the basic instincts and emotions of the customer have changed. These are as reliable and as constant as the sun and the moon. Advertising and products or services directed to these instincts and emotions will get results as long as man inhabits the earth. However, these current trends in the way people think will be of value to you in preparing your advertising materials. All in all, these trends make your job easier because the customer is more willing to buy.

2

Getting Started
Step-by-Step

The actual mechanics of starting a new mail order business are not that difficult. Of course, the steps should be properly planned so they move forward smoothly and dovetail efficiently. To introduce you to a proven simple plan which enables you to get started with no lost motion, an operational flow diagram is illustrated in figure 2-1.

This diagram shows the major operations in separate blocks, logically arranged. Blocks stacked vertically show those operations which occur essentially at the same time. The sequence and flow of operations is indicated by the arrows connecting the various blocks. The initial operation (choosing a product or service) is at the left end and, as time passes, operations further to the right are scheduled for action. This flow diagram is planned to control the many different steps required in getting your new mail order business started efficiently and rapidly.

The flow diagram is presented early in the book to demonstrate that starting a new business is actually a very simple and easy process when done properly. Each operation in the flow diagram is fully described in the remaining chapters of this book, and full instructions are given to guide your actions every step of the way.

The following brief description of starting your new mail order business is based upon the operational flow diagram. Refer to this diagram as you read it now, but don't let unfamiliar terms or operations confuse you. They are fully described in later chapters and as you study the remaining chapters, each one will become clear to you. A number of technical terms whose use could not be avoided are further defined in the Glossary at the back of this book.

Stage 1—The first step, of course, is to determine what kind of business

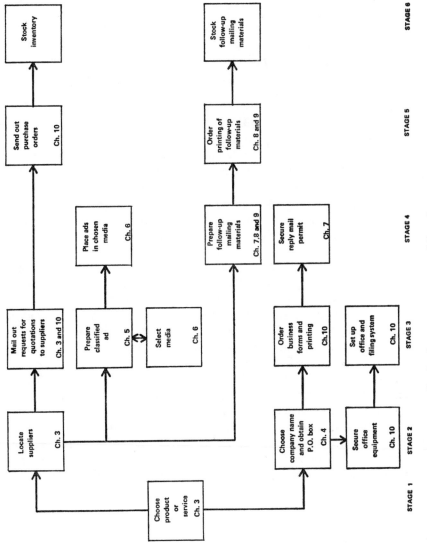

Fig. 2-1 Setting up your mail order business: operational flow diagram.

STAGE 1 STAGE 2 STAGE 3 STAGE 4 STAGE 5 STAGE 6

Choose product or service Ch. 3

Locate suppliers Ch. 3

Mail out requests for quotations to suppliers Ch. 3 and 10

Send out purchase orders Ch. 10

Stock inventory

Prepare classified ad Ch. 5

Select media Ch. 6

Place ads in chosen media Ch. 6

Choose company name and obtain P.O. box Ch. 4

Secure office equipment Ch. 10

Order business forms and printing Ch.10

Set up office and filing system Ch. 10

Prepare follow-up mailing materials Ch. 7,8 and 9

Secure reply mail permit Ch. 7

Order printing of follow-up materials Ch. 8 and 9

Stock follow-up mailing materials

you want to own, the product or service upon which you will base your operation (chapter 3). After doing a little research and thinking, assume that you have decided upon a product called a "widget." You feel many people will buy widgets, based on your understanding of the customer, as discussed in the previous chapter.

Stage 2—Now that you've selected widgets as your product, you need to locate manufacturers of widgets (chapter 3). The easiest way of doing this is to look in *Thomas Register* at your public library, under the classification "Widgets." Copy all these names and addresses. These represent possible suppliers of the widgets you intend to sell. (*Thomas Register* is an alphabetical guide to products and manufacturers, and is a storehouse of information for the mail order businessperson.)

Now choose a name for your company and get a post office box (chapter 4) and start gathering the office equipment you will need (chapter 10).

Stage 3—Contact the various magazines and/or newspapers in which you intend to place classified ads (chapter 6) and prepare an effective ad (chapter 5). Mail out requests for quotation (chapters 3 and 10) to potential widget suppliers. While setting up your office and filing system (chapter 10), order letterheads and the blank business forms you need (also chapter 10).

Stage 4—Begin preparing the mailing pieces (chapters 7-9) you will send to all who reply to your ads. Place your classified ads in selected media (chapter 6), and secure your business reply permit (chapter 7).

Stage 5—Order your follow-up mailing materials from your printer (chapter 8). When the quotations come in, choose the suppliers you intend to use and place orders with them by purchase orders (chapter 10).

Stage 6—Store the follow-up mailing pieces received from your printer to await replies to your classified ads. When your shipment of widgets arrives, store them ready to mail to your customers.

This is how your mail order business is started. You are now ready to fill your customers' orders as they come in. Handling of replies to your ads, processing orders, and the control of your operations are discussed in chapter 11. Additional flow diagrams included in later chapters guide you in every step of order processing, filing, paying your bills, and record keeping.

3

Choosing a Product or Service that Sells

WHAT YOU SELL IS YOUR BUSINESS

Your product or service *is* your business. Even with the best and most effective advertising and distribution and the lowest prices, *what you sell determines the extent to which you will succeed or fail.* Choice of a suitable—and saleable—product or service is the most important aspect of every mail order company. It is worth every bit of thought you can give.

A successful product for mail order sales is often different from those found in stores. The differences in merchandising techniques require a different approach to choosing a suitable product. It is not merely wrapped and handed across the counter; it must be mailed to the customer, passing through many hands and often being knocked about, dropped, or crushed. *It must easily be sold at a price far above its cost* so that your business expenses will be covered with enough left over to provide a profit. Mailing costs should be as low as possible. And on top of all this, your product should give the customer more than he expects to receive in benefits—if you want him to keep being a customer, that is.

SEARCHING FOR A PRODUCT

It is not as difficult as it might at first appear to find a suitable product. There is room for mail order sales of products within almost every category you can think of. Read the classified and display ads in magazines like *Popular Mechanics, Salesman Opportunity* (a fertile source for all kinds of unusual products), and others which carry many pages of ads.

Note the many different products and services which are offered to the reader. Look over six months or so of back issues of these magazines at your public library and *see how many of these same ads appear, month after month*. These products are selling! You can bet that if they weren't, the ads would soon disappear. No one spends money to advertise a product no one will buy, at least, not after this sad fact is discovered.

Check the ads which interest you and send for information. (Keep an account of the money you spend for magazines, postage, envelopes, stationery, and postcards. These are legitimate business expenses and are deductible on your tax return as market or product research.) You will very shortly be deluged with advertising matter. Study each mailing piece in the light of the product for sale. Some will be effective and some will be boring or insulting. Remember the good ideas you run across and file these advertisements for future reference. You may be able to adapt them to your own product.

In your search for a suitable mail order product or service, read the yellow pages in any large city telephone directory (available at telephone company offices and in many public libraries). Browse through book stores, variety stores, hardware and auto supply stores, sporting goods stores, gift shops, hobby shops, etc. Get on as many mailing lists as possible (the *Direct Mail/Marketing Association*, 6 East 43rd Street, New York, NY 10017, will be pleased to accommodate your request without charge) to see what others are offering. Pore through the several volumes of *Thomas Register* at your public library. Ads placed under "Agents Wanted" or "Business Opportunities" often offer products suitable for mail order merchandising. Don't neglect these classifications when reading the newspapers. In short, keep your eyes open as you read and shop. You will soon have discovered so many possible mail order products that your biggest problem will be to decide which one or more to choose as the cornerstone of your business.

THE IDEAL MAIL ORDER PRODUCT

When deciding among several possible products, keep in mind that mail order sales require certain qualities in a product not essential to other methods of merchandising. The *theoretically ideal* mail order product would sell to men, women, and children and generate repeat orders. If you can discover this product, your fortune is made.

The ideal mail order product should possess as many of the following qualities as possible. It should:

Be attractive
Be useful
Be needed every day

Be used by young and old, male and female
Wear out or be used up and require replacement
Sell for much more than it costs to produce
Be unbreakable
Require no special packaging or handling
Be of obvious high quality materials and workmanship
Be mailable for a few pennies
Be unique and available nowhere else
Be an honest bargain when compared to competitive products
Give the customer more for his money than he expects
Appeal to instincts and basic drives
Improve the customer materially, socially, or emotionally
Be indispensable—no home should be without one or, preferably, several

So far no one has discovered the ideal product (although a simple bar of toilet soap comes close). The ideal product may not even exist, but with luck and persistent effort you should be able to approach the ideal. You can reduce the effort involved in deciding upon a product by investigating only products in those categories which appeal to you *and* meet many of the requirements listed above.

If you find a product advertised which appears to have good sales potential, buy a sample. (The cost is tax deductible.) Check its quality, mailability, and how many of the characteristics of the ideal mail order product it fulfills. If it passes inspection, write to the manufacturer and get prices and shipping details. The manufacturer's name will be somewhere on the product or the packaging (if it isn't, write to whom you bought it from and find out).

No product is ideal, of course, unless you can sell it at a profitable price. So pricing must be part of your thinking as you select a product or service. Based on the manufacturer's prices, estimate your total costs per unit and compare this with what you feel you could sell it for (pricing is discussed further in chapter 4). Don't forget to add an estimated portion of the costs of packing, postage, utilities, rent, depreciation on office machines and furnishings, advertising, etc. to the cost of the product. Add in a reasonable profit and compare this with your estimated selling price. You may be able to sell for less than you estimated, or make a larger profit selling at your estimated price.

RECOMMENDED PRODUCTS AND SERVICES

Many suitable types of products and services for effective and successful merchandising by mail order are discussed in the following pages. These represent the result of considerable research into mail order merchandising. The categories covered in this chapter are as complete as is possible. Specific types of products in each category are discussed separately since *not* all products in all categories will be suitable mail order items.

Before going into the *recommended* products and services, though, first a word about a type of business *not* to go into. *Do not* involve yourself in selling materials which your customer is to process and which you guarantee to buy back from him. Your customer has no understanding of the difference between gross and net profit. To him, profit is profit and he cannot be convinced differently. Nor is he aware of the legitimate price spread in the manufacturer-wholesaler-distributor-dealer relationship. He will call your legitimate wholesale price offer a fraud and you a cheat, for if a similar item costs $2 at retail, he expects you to pay him $2. Your 50¢ wholesale price offer will be angrily rejected. You will lose a customer and by his vocal complaints you will lose other potential customers. He is also likely to write accusatory letters to the Better Business Bureau or the Federal Trade Commission. While these will cause you no actual damage if your business and pricing structure are honest and fair, it will cost you in time and money to satisfy the inquiries by these organizations. Confine your activities to selling *to* your customer. Do not buy *from* him.

Below are some ideas of mail order businesses you *can* go into.

GENERAL BOOKS

Advantages—Books are a high-profit item, usually obtainable from the publisher at 40 percent or more off the list price. Unsold books can sometimes be returned to the publisher for credit. Mailing costs are very low at the special fourth class rate. Packaging is easy and inexpensive. Books are available in many price ranges and on every imaginable subject. New books appear on the market every month. Paperback books especially are available at quantity discounts.

Disadvantages—There is much competition in book selling. Books are also available locally to the customer. There are a number of mail order companies specializing in books. Books which do not sell in the book stores are "remaindered," that is, sold at enormous discounts to large companies like Marboro Books and Publishers Central Bureau who mail out comprehensive catalogs offering these books at extremely low prices.

Customer viewpoint—Many books are sold by mail, especially art books, soft and hard core pornography, and other specialized books generally unavailable in stores. Your potential customer rarely visits book stores. He usually will use the library when information is needed in a hurry. He watches television in preference to reading novels. He will normally buy only those books within his fields of interest, work, or hobby.

Suggestions—The beginner should probably avoid general types of books available from other sources. Books on special interest subjects, some of which are considered below, may be offered as a profitable sideline by an established mail order dealer. Books and pamphlets over which you control distribution by ownership of the copyright and covering subjects in which the customer is or can be interested, are excellent. Printing and other costs are low and profits are high. Properly chosen, a small line of unique books and pamphlets can support a very profitable enterprise.

HOW-TO BOOKS

Advantages—The words how-to sell a lot of books. This variety of book promises an easy road to desired knowledge or skill. Almost any subject you can think of will make a book and most of them will sell reasonably well. They are low in cost and can often justify a much higher price than their bulk would suggest. These books sell because they promise so many desirable things to the customer. Packing costs and postage are low. Printing and binding need not be expensive. If *you* can write suitable books yourself or pay a writer to prepare useful manuscripts for you so that they are available only from you, you're even better off.

Disadvantages—The same disadvantages for general books apply to how-to books if you sell books purchased from the publisher. There are *no* significant *disadvantages if you control the copyright for the books you sell,* either by writing them yourself or having them written for you.

Customer viewpoint—The same viewpoint expressed for general books applies.

Suggestions—How-to books purchased wholesale from a publisher make a good sideline for an established mail order dealer. For instance, a dealer in automotive accessories can also sell automotive books. One who sells sporting or recreational goods can also sell books about sports, games, and travel. To be the primary product the dealer sells, the books should be available only from him. He should control the copyright as mentioned above. Following is a partial selection of suitable topics for how-to books. You can probably think of many more.

Travel guides
Hunting, fishing, camping
Boating, sailing, cruising, canoeing
Sports (skiing, golf, archery, tennis, bowling)
Cars (customizing, tuning, hopping up, rebuilding)
Vacation guides (routes, motels, restaurants, prices)
Furniture (building, refinishing, upholstering)
Houses (buying, decorating, repairs)
Gardening (flowers, fruit, vegetables, lawns)
Musical instruments (playing, building, repairing)

Power tools (setting up a workshop, using tools)
Theater (stage sets, designing costumes)
Health (weight control, exercises, diets)
Beauty (make-up, fashions, accessories, hair styling)
Lamps (making from bottles, wiring, shades)
Jewelry (making, cutting and polishing stones)
Collecting (anything can be collected)
Models (ships, planes, automobiles, spacecraft, missiles)
Upholstery (how to, cleaning, repairing)
Animals, pets (raising, grooming, training, breeding)
Hobbies (every hobby can support another book)
Clothing (sewing, knitting, crocheting, tailoring)
Printing (setting up shop, getting business)
Auctions (how to buy, recognizing bargains)
Antiques (recognizing fakes, values)
Saving money (buying at lowest prices)
Cooking (family recipes, wild foods, unusual dishes)
Liquor (new drinks, unusual drinks)
Bookkeeping (simplified, accurate methods)
Repairs (appliances, toys, cars, furniture)
Something for nothing (useful articles from junk)
Treasure (where it is, finding it, legal aspects)
Flower arrangements (fresh, dried)
Semiprecious stones (finding, recognizing, polishing, setting, making jewelry)

Travel Books

Advantages—The same advantages apply to travel books as are listed for general books. In addition, more people have the desire to travel and the money to do so. They are in the market for travel books.

Disadvantages—The same disadvantages apply as for general books.

Customer viewpoint—The same conditions as for general books apply to travel books. Too, there are many travel agencies which provide free material. If your books appeal to the customer's special interests he will buy them. You must rely greatly on your advertising.

Suggestions—Consider general travel books as strictly a sideline if you sell them at all. Travel books alone will rarely support your whole operation, although there are mail order companies which sell only such books and have been doing well for years. Search out specialized books in this field, especially those which promote budget travel and how to see all the sights for the minimum amount of money. Try to find items which offer information directed to certain groups such as single men or women, those over 50, religious groups, retired persons, etc. Tell your customer plainly in your advertising what your books will do for *him*.

BOOKS OF INTEREST TO WOMEN

Advantages—This is an excellent and uncrowded field. Women today are much more likely to assert their individuality and independence. They are doing many more things now which formerly they depended upon men to do for them. Because of this, women will buy books which show them how to accomplish tasks which are new to them. Especially if you control the copyright by writing them or having them written for you, such books and pamphlets will easily support a successful and fast-growing mail order operation. Production and mailing costs are low. Your selling prices can far exceed your costs, assuring you of a high profit. With booklets on several related subjects for sale, you will get repeat orders. Women will tell their friends about your books, and you can expect additional orders from them.

Disadvantages—The only disadvantage is that by appealing only to women you effectively cut the possible number of potential customers in half, though some men will buy your books for their wives or women friends.

Customer viewpoint—The woman customer is wholly receptive to well-written and well-illustrated instruction booklets which teach her new skills. There are few of these currently available and she will readily buy new ones as they appear. She wants and needs such sources of information. However, she demands that both the written instructions and the accompanying illustrations be clear and easily understood. Above all, they must work!

Suggestions—The care and repair of almost anything a woman owns or uses, and additional outlets for her energy and spare time activities, provide almost unlimited sources of ideas for instruction booklets. Below is a partial list of suitable subjects for instruction booklets intended for women. You will probably think of many more yourself.

Household appliances
Her automobile, motorcycle, or bicycle
Furnishings
Decorating ideas
Clothing and accessories
Working at home for extra income
Hair styling
Make-up
Refinishing furniture
Upholstering
Plumbing repairs
Adjustment of stoves and ovens
Heating system repairs

Air conditioner adjustment and maintenance
New uses for foods in simple recipes
Sewing, knitting, crocheting, and tatting
Childcare
Learning new sports and games
Music and musical instruments
Foreign languages
Growing house plants, flowers, and vegetables
Canning and preservation of foods
Breeding, grooming, and showing animals
Horsemanship
Making lamps
Simple radio and television repairs
More efficient methods of doing housework
Jewelry making
Making shelves and cabinets
Roof repair
House painting (interior and exterior)
Repairing plaster walls
Repairing stairs, porches, and steps
Replacing window panes
Installing locks
Hanging doors
Installing floor and ceiling tiles
Installing wall-to-wall carpet
Cleaning drapes, carpets, and furniture
Landscaping
Growing dwarf fruits and vegetables
Insulating walls and attics
Building fireplaces and barbecues
Installing outdoor lighting
Eliminating insects and rodents

CONSTRUCTION PLANS

Advantages—If you draw up your own plans or have them made for you by a draftsman, they can be obtained only from you. They cost pennies per copy and sell for dollars. The lack of good carpenters, plumbers, and mechanics at low wages has made everyone aware of the benefits of do-it-yourself methods. Your customer wants things done and needs only to be shown how to do them simply and at the least cost. He also lacks the skill of experts and needs plans and instructions so simple and clear that the job practically does itself. A stock of plans for several commonly wanted projects will sell very well.

Disadvantages—There are many companies selling plans for almost anything you can think of. This competition means the plans you devise must make the job *easier, quicker, cheaper,* or *better* than others available. Your advertising must stress this.

Customer viewpoint—Your customer needs and wants plans for practically everything. He is willing to pay from $2 to $5 and even $10 for a set of plans, but seldom more. It depends on the cost of his materials and the value of what he makes or repairs. Your advertising must convince him that your plans will best solve his problems with the least effort and at the lowest cost.

Suggestions—Construction plans support several mail order businesses. They are also an excellent sideline if you carry how-to-books. The fields of interest are practically unlimited: Sporting equipment, camping gear, radio, hi-fi stereo equipment, burglar and fire alarm systems, furniture, built-ins, plumbing, automotive conversion, swimming and fish pools, patios, septic tanks, cement work, etc. This can be a fertile field for you and plans can be mailed in envelopes at third class rates. Plans also require little space for your stock. Plans should be copyrighted and you should control their distribution, if possible.

NOVELTIES

Advantages—Novelties which catch the public's interest will have skyrocketing sales. They are inexpensive and will support large profit margins. Most are imported. Some possess a quality which will enable them to sell for years, though most do not. There is always a profit for the seller who is first to offer popular novelties to the public.

Disadvantages—Most novelties have a short sales life. You may be left with a large inventory which you cannot sell profitably. When the public starts to buy novelties you cannot sit back and waste time; you must move fast and get the merchandise into your customer's hands. You must be able to second-guess the public so you will have on hand the next thing he is apt to want. Fads come and go (remember the hula hoop) and the public loses interest rapidly. It is extremely difficult to foretell the future interests of the customer.

Customer viewpoint—Your customer doesn't know what he wants until he sees or hears of it. If it is considered stylish, fun, or different (way out!) he is likely to buy and will swamp you with orders. He loses interest rapidly, though, once the novelty has worn off or "everybody has one."

Suggestions—Magic tricks, both the simple instructions and plans which can be mailed in an envelope and small devices themselves, have a strong appeal and a continuing market, especially among juveniles. This product supports several mail order companies which earn good money. Current interest in "executive toys," gimmicks for the busy executive to keep on his desk, is also evident. Such perennial favorites as nameplates, personalized items of all kinds, pipes, lighters, smoking accessories, trophies, all have steady sales. If the product also has a practical use or a prestige value, it will have a longer sales life than the item whose only interest is its novelty.

Sporting Goods and Supplies

Advantages—There is a large and expanding market in the field of sporting goods, much of which is mail-order serviced. Profits can be high and costs low. A very broad line of products can be offered, especially if your wholesale suppliers will drop ship your merchandise (discussed in chapter 12). Your products rarely become outdated.

Disadvantages—There is competition from local sporting goods stores near the customer and a large number of mail order companies in this field, although most of the latter specialize in one or two items. You will have to watch quality, service, cost, and sales appeal very closely.

Customer viewpoint—The love of the outdoors, an interest in hunting, fishing, and camping, in woods, fields, and streams, is a deep instinct in man. Most men find it hard to resist buying books and equipment in this field, even if they know they probably will never have a chance to really use them. Whole families are now avid campers and hikers, especially since the advent of motorhomes and pick-up camper vehicles. Trail bikes and snowmobiles are being purchased and used by increasing numbers of families. Boating is a major and expanding family activity and love of the sea is as old as mankind.

A very large number of goods and accessories is purchased by mail. The numerous classified and display ads in such magazines as *Argosy, Field & Stream, Outdoor Life, Yachting, Motor Boating and Sailing, Sea,* plus the numerous magazines appealing to campers, snowmobilers, etc. indicate widespread public interest and will give you an idea of the wide range of products sold by mail.

Suggestions—Choose a particular field such as boating, fishing, or camping and stick to it. The boating market is very large and receptive to high-quality merchandise at reasonable prices. Most of what is offered for use on boats seems to be far overpriced. If you can offer high quality products at lower than market prices—and this should be very easy to do—your profits will expand rapidly in this field.

The same is true in accessories for campers and recreational vehicles. Practically everything offered is priced very high, apparently not based on cost plus a reasonable profit margin, but on what the market can be made to pay. This is not dishonest, it's capitalism in action. However, it does represent a great opportunity for a person willing to accept a more normal-sized profit and enjoy huge volume sales.

There is actually no *real* competition in the boating and recreational vehicle accessory and equipment fields due to this tendency to mark up everything far beyond its actual cost at wholesale.

Study the needs and desires of persons in the field you choose. Find out what is presently available which can satisfy these needs and desires. Check both the costs to you and the usual market price. You will undoubtedly find some products which you can handle at a good but not excessive profit, selling it for less than similar items available elsewhere.

TOYS

Advantages—The population is expanding and so is the market. Toys are usually inexpensive and can be sold at good profits. Novel toys will bring more sales than year-by-year standbys. Toys for babies and toddlers represent large sales potentials and are not troubled as greatly by competition from stores as are toys for older children. Toy manufacturers will often dropship for you so you will have no inventory and no mailing expenses. The market is steady and not seasonal, except for the pre-Christmas rush.—

Disadvantages—Most of your competition will come from counter sales in existing stores. New developments in toys may reduce your sales prospects.

Customer viewpoint—Because of the mobility of the American public, families are usually scattered. Grandparents, uncles, and aunts have to mail gift toys to the children in the family; they prefer to order by mail and let the supplier (you) handle the shipping problems. Too, many families prefer to purchase toys by mail, especially toys which may not be readily available in nearby towns. Rural and small town families very often do a considerable amount of their shopping by mail.

Suggestions—The best toy is one which retail stores do not or will not carry. Toys that do something, those that have moving parts, sell more readily than immobile toys, although soft, cuddly animals are a constant source of sales. Toys must be sturdily built, and not have any sharp points or edges, lead-based paints, or small parts which might easily become detached. They should be sanitary and fire resistant. Supplies such as doll clothes and furniture are good sales items if you can secure them at low cost. Toys may be combined with novelties to provide steady sales and good profits.

Children like to play in dirt, mud, and water, and toys to help them have fun in these environments will find buyers. Children also love to pretend to be adults, and toys and props which cater to this fantasy will sell well. This is especially true if they are unusual and different from those available locally. Toys which reflect the space age are particularly good sellers.

Remember—*children don't buy toys; adults buy them*. So cater to the child in the adult; attract the *adult* in your ads and with your toys.

Burglar and Fire Protection

Advantages—Crime is rising at an alarming rate, especially burglaries. People no longer feel safe in their homes. Cold weather brings an increase in home fires. There are numerous manufacturers of alarm systems, some of which are simple enough for anyone to install. Your customer is receptive to an alarm system which will not cost too much, is easy for him to install, and which offers to protect him from losing what he already owns. Remember—*he is much more interested in keeping what he has than in acquiring more.* Both the size of the market and the number of suppliers is increasing. There is excellent profit potential in this field in the foreseeable future.

Disadvantages—The customer is slow to act. He thinks "it can't happen to me" and doubts his own ability to install even a simple alarm. You will have to convince him with your advertising and get him to act. This can be difficult. You should stress the simplicity of the installation and how detailed and clear the printed installation instructions are. Your advertising will have to play upon his fears of loss, and fright advertising can be tricky.

Customer viewpoint—Your customer is afraid but tends to disregard the likelihood of a personal disaster. If he is convinced not only that an alarm will give him protection but that he can actually install it himself, he will buy. He tends to blame fate for bad luck, not admitting that he could have prevented his troubles with a little foresight. He wants to believe he can do something for his own protection.

Suggestions—This field includes not only alarms for various potential events but associated products like fire extinguishers for home, auto, and boat, locks for doors and windows, fireproof storage boxes for documents, and small safes, to name a few. Look over what is available. You may find a number of saleable products which you can handle. If you have any electrical or electronic training, you will do well to design your own alarm system, which may be patentable; as a minimum you can copyright the installation diagrams and instructions and control the distribution of your own alarm system.

If you have a key-making machine you can add the making of duplicate keys to your service. However, certain types of keys may not be legally duplicated—safe deposit box keys, for example—so check with an attorney or the local law enforcement agencies for exact information. Such a key-making service is primarily used to provide extra keys for the customer at the time of sale of the safety device, since he can usually have keys made locally and will not use a mail order service for keys alone.

Automotive Accessories

Advantages—There are millions of automobile owners. Most people are very much interested in anything that makes the car look better, run better, be more comfortable in use, use less gasoline or oil, start better in cold weather, produce more horsepower, retain a high resale value, reduce repairs, etc. There are good profits to be made in this field with the proper products and advertising.

Disadvantages—There is considerable competition. Your product absolutely has to be unique or, if it is available from others, yours will have to do more and cost the customer less money.

Customer viewpoint—The customer demands that you prove your claims to his satisfaction. He often knows quite a bit about automobiles and can spot a phony claim a mile away. He will buy if you can convince him your product can deliver what he wants.

Suggestions—There are thousands of products available, including automotive novelties which make a good sideline. You should be fairly familiar with automobiles if you expect to be successful with automotive products. Buy sample products and test them on your own automobile. Manufacturers' claims are often exaggerated, to apply the kindest interpretation. Read the many auto magazines and don't forget to *read all the ads*. Try to work out a drop-ship arrangement (see chapter 12) with your supplier so you will not have to tie up money in a stock of merchandise.

FORMULAS AND RECIPES

Advantages—Everyone likes to save money. Many products which are the "same" as the expensive, widely advertised brand name goods can be made by the customer for pennies. Your stock is printed paper and your product is delivered to your customer in ordinary envelopes at very low mailing costs. You can handle a large variety of different formulas with little increase in your costs. You can also expand your business by mixing your own products under your private label and selling them by mail.

Disadvantages—Books of formulas are on the shelves of many public libraries and a few are sold by mail. Unless the customer can save a large amount of money he may not be willing to bother. Not all ingredients are always available in the smaller towns.

Customer viewpoint—The customer will not usually be willing to make such simple and widely available products as soap, cosmetics, or toiletries. He is a little afraid of the word "chemicals" and does not understand nor realize that everything he eats, drinks, and wears is made up of chemicals as is his own body. He is interested in saving dollars but tends to ignore the pennies. As an example, he will go to the trouble of making beer and wine at home since taxes make these drinks costly. A number of mail order companies sell instruction booklets for making such beverages. Their ads appear every month and they are making money all year long.

Suggestions—Buy a book of formulas or borrow one from the library.

Read through it, looking for suitable formulas. The book will be copyrighted, so before you simply copy any of its formulas to reproduce for sale, check with an attorney. Many such formulas, although appearing in a copyrighted book, are actually in the public domain and can be reproduced and sold by anyone. Others may be protected under copyright and in this case permission of the copyright owner must be obtained before you can republish them for sale. In any case, it will be best to reword the instructions accompanying each formula you use. This makes your product appear different from others using the same formula. Be sure to copyright *your* printed material.

If you intend to mix your own private label products for sale, do not even consider medicines, tonics, cosmetics, or any product applied to the human body, internally or externally. This is a direct invitation to trouble from the Food and Drug Administration. You can safely offer these formulas for sale, of course.

If you sell your own product, do not sell its formula, or you will be in direct competition with yourself. This is a sure way to lose money in a hurry.

Small booklets or pamphlets selling for $1, $2, or $3 will be more profitable and easier to sell than single formulas with mixing and using directions. All the formulas in each booklet should be related to each other, such as 12 beer recipes or 24 homemade wines. A bonus offer of a few similar formulas can be made in your advertising as a reward for promptness in ordering your booklet or product. This must be absolutely free, with no strings attached. If some ingredients or special equipment are hard for the customer to locate, you should sell these as well.

SEMIPRECIOUS STONES

Advantages—A large and growing number of people are rockhounds— hobbyists who go into the field looking for attractive stones which can be made into jewelry. Many of these stones are classified as semiprecious because of their rarity and beauty. People gather these stones, cut and polish them, and make them into bracelets, rings, brooches, necklaces, etc. Anyone can learn to make attractive and valuable jewelry of original design with little skill, effort, or expense. The number of people interested in stones and jewelry-making is growing rapidly, even in areas where natural stones are hard to find or nonexistent. They will buy stones (rough and polished), jewelry findings (the metal parts of rings, pins, bracelets, etc.), abrasives, polishing and cutting machines, etc. There are very high profits to be made if you live where you can go out and pick up the raw stones in streams or fields. The desert and mountain states have many naturally occurring minerals which polish into beautiful gems. If you live there, stones are free for the gathering. Your stock will not spoil or ever be out of date.

Disadvantages—If you have to purchase raw stones in bulk and cannot gather them free of charge, your profits cannot be as great, though you can still make good money. Your shipping costs will be greater because of the weight of your product. There is competition from dealers whose source of stones is free.

Customer viewpoint—Your customer is interested in unusual jewelry, one-of-a-kind pieces. Prices are high for finished pieces but low for stones and findings from which unique jewelry can be made. The customer is attracted by these savings. He can buy a tumbler for about $10 and his other supplies cost little, so he can have an interesting and inexpensive hobby with which he can produce valuable, original jewelry. Since machines do all the work even when he isn't present (tumblers must operate for many hours to properly polish stones), he finds this is a great advantage. He is attracted by low cost, the minimum of effort and skill required, and the opportunity to create something of beauty which is also practical and unique.

Suggestions—Look over several copies of the various rockhound magazines such as *Gems and Minerals, Lapidary Journal,* and *Rockhound,* or subscribe to one or more. *Read the ads* as well as the articles. Answer some of the ads, particularly those offering information or instruction. If you live where stones can be picked up free, buy a selection of rough stones so you will know what to look for in the field. Buy a geologist's hammer and gather your own stones. Learn all you can. Buy a tumbler and polish some stones. In fact, you will probably end up making jewelry which you can also offer for sale.

This field lends itself well to carrying a complete line of equipment: tumblers, saws, tools, rough stones, polished stones, jewelry findings, abrasive powders, ivory nuts (used for polishing), solder, pitch, instruction booklets, and completed jewelry.

Your ads for parts and equipment will reach more persons interested in rocks and jewelry if you place them in the various rockhound magazines, and thus the ads will be more productive of sales. However, if you sell finished jewelry, your ads should be placed in consumer magazines and women's magazines. Ads for polished stones and findings—do-it-yourself jewelry kits—will draw well in hobby and women's magazines and in Sunday supplements to metropolitan newspapers.

While there are healthy profits to be made selling equipment your greatest profit potential and one which is continued by repeat business is in rough and polished stones, polishing grits, ivory nuts, tumbler liners (they wear out fairly rapidly), jewelry findings. Your customers *use these up and have to purchase more;* make sure they can get them from you!

Rough stones can be purchased in hundred pound and larger lots and delivered by freight. Prices are low. You can grade these by size and separate them by type, repackaging for retail sale in one-, two- and five-pound bags. Abrasive grits and ivory nuts should also be bought in bulk and repackaged for retail sale at a considerable profit.

You can also make up sets of rough stones for sale to beginning rockhounds. Each stone must be plainly identified such as jasper, agate, rose quartz, beryl, etc. Sets of polished stones can also be sold for display pieces and for mounting in findings.

REPACKAGING

Advantages—Whatever people generally buy or need in small quantities but are usually sold in bulk or fairly large quantities can be repackaged inexpensively and sold at a good profit. This idea is adaptable to everything from buttons or screws to transistors or neckties. Kits of different but related items also make for profitable sales. Most people prefer to buy attractively packaged small quantities of such things as hardware, fish hooks, electronic parts, etc. They are also attracted by made-up kits of useful items. The items you repackage for individual sale can be purchased very inexpensively in bulk by the pound, gross, or case. Plastic boxes and bags used for repackaging may also be bought inexpensively in large quantities.

Disadvantages—There may be competition for some items from stores near the customer. In specialized fields like electronics you will have competition from established companies with massive buying power and years of experience such as Radio Shack, Lafayette Radio, etc.

Customer viewpoint—The customer is attracted by the convenience of being able to buy only a small number of an item instead of a whole box, and he disregards the higher cost per unit which he pays for this convenience. He would much rather pay a quarter for ten screws in a store than a dollar for a gross, since he doesn't need a gross. Too, he likes the idea of being able to buy several sizes or kinds of an item for little more than a standard box of one size or kind. It takes little effort to get his order if you offer something he wants or needs, attractively packaged and at a low price compared to the usual box or standard package.

Suggestions—Screws; safety pins; sinkers; fish hook assortments; nuts; bolts; washers; assorted buttons; spices and herbs; greeting cards; electronic parts; curtain hardware; brass parts for flush toilet mechanism repair; faucet washers and screws; hose washers and fittings; paper clips; paper fasteners; ballpoint pens in colors; pen refills; rubber bands; balloons; spools of thread; needle assortments; marbles; corks; etc. Almost anything you can think of will lend itself to repackaging.

Also consider making up kits for special purposes: disposable wash-up kits for auto travel; first aid kits made up especially for auto, camping, boating, backpacking, etc.; emergency rainwear in thin plastic; hangover remedies; civil defense-type survival kits; the opportunities are endless.

Take a walk through a variety or department store and note how many different items are packaged in small quantities in glassine bags and bubble packs on cards. Read the ads in several of the sporting or men's magazines. Note the prices and quantities offered and compare this with bulk prices. (*Thomas Register* is the publication to check when searching for bulk suppliers; it may be found in most public libraries, and many local manufacturing businesses will have their own copies which they may let you look through.) The difference between bulk and repackaged retail prices can be almost all net profit.

CONFIDENTIAL REMAIL, FORWARDING, AND SECRET ADDRESS

Advantages—There are many customers willing to pay you for practically no work at all, merely because you live where you do and not where they do. You have practically no overhead expenses. You need no more than a small table and chair to conduct this business. Monthly classified ads are your only expense. This can be your entire business, especially if you have an exotic or unusual address, or a very profitable sideline to your main mail order business. Almost every cent which comes in is profit.

Disadvantages—This business will rarely earn a great deal of money unless you live in a large city, a resort area, a historical town, or foreign country. There is competition from other mail order advertisers offering this service. However, unless there is a competitor living in your town, you may safely ignore such competition.

Customer viewpoint—Many people like to pretend they are elsewhere and will gladly pay a quarter or more to have a letter, which they have sealed and stamped, postmarked in your town or city. Others want no one to know where they actually are and pay three to five dollars to you each month to use your address for their incoming and outgoing mail, supplying their own stamps. Others want special services for which they are willing to pay even more.

Suggestions—The motives of your customers for not wanting others to know their whereabouts are none of your business. You are merely providing a completely legal service in good faith and have no knowledge of the contents of the mail you handle for forwarding or remailing.

Remailing usually earns 25¢ to 35¢ per letter you handle. You merely remove the addressed and stamped envelope from the one in which it was delivered to you and add it to your outgoing mail.

Ordinary mail forwarding on a monthly fee basis, usually about $3, requires you to scratch out your address on the incoming envelope, add the customer's address, rubber stamp it with the words *Please Forward* and add it to your outgoing mail.

Confidential mail forwarding or a confidential address requires you to place the incoming envelope, unopened, into one of your own envelopes or a blank envelope, sealing, stamping, addressing and mailing it. This should bring in at least 25¢ per letter plus the cost of postage and plus a monthly fee which can exceed $3 because of the confidentiality of this method and because of the extra work and materials involved.

All incoming letters for confidential remail forwarding to one address in one day can be mailed together in a single envelope at a savings in postage to you, though you should charge the customer for separate postage for each letter forwarded to him.

It is often advantageous but not necessary to rent a post office box for your mail forwarding business.

RESEARCH AND INFORMATION SERVICE

Advantages—You have practically no overhead. Your fees are based on the time you spend securing the information desired by your customer and upon the difficulty in securing it. Rates generally should be $3 to $5 per hour for most types of research. A large number of people either do not know how or are too lazy or busy to find out what they wish to know. Such services are used often by freelance writers. If you live in a large city with a good public library or have access to a college or university library, research can be a profitable business for you.

Disadvantages—There is some competition from other researchers but much less than you might imagine. Unless you have access to a large, comprehensive library you will not be able to make a living as a researcher though it may still be a good sideline business.

Customer viewpoint—The customer often lacks knowledge or inclination to dig up the facts he needs. He is willing to pay for this service if he needs the information badly enough. Often all he wants is specific information regarding your area because he is being transferred there or is thinking of moving there.

Suggestions—Advertise in the classified sections of several large circulation newspapers throughout the country, possibly including Canada. Include the newspapers in your own city. Also place occasional classified ads in writer's magazines, mechanics and men's magazines, and in *Saturday Review*.

Learn how to find information in your library. Understand the numbering system (usually Dewey decimal or Library of Congress) used to identify the different categories of books in your library. Know how to use the card catalog. When researching, take notes or use a tape recorder if this is allowed. Type up your report at home, making one or more copies for your files. Mail the original report to your customer with your bill. Try to get a deposit from the customer *before* doing any work for him and bill him or refund the difference with your report.

Retain copies of each research report. Someone else will want the same information and you can often satisfy his needs with the same or with little additional information. You should charge your normal fees just as if you had to search out the information for him.

You may charge by the hour or by the page, but give your customer good value for his money. If he is satisfied he will return to you from time to time in the future, and may also recommend you to friends and colleagues.

EMPLOYMENT INFORMATION

Advantages—Overhead is very low. The information you sell can be obtained free or for very low costs. Mailing costs are low since your "product" is sheets of printed or mimeographed paper. There is a constant market with a high profit potential. Because your selling price can be reasonably low you can sell directly from your classified ads and not need any additional follow-up mailing pieces. There is probably little or no competition where you live.

Disadvantages—Usually this service must be combined with some other product or service to increase your income, although some mail order companies sell only employment information, usually covering jobs in foreign lands.

Customer viewpoint—Your customer believes the grass is always greener somewhere else. A majority of families are willing to move if better jobs or climate are in prospect. America has a mobile population. People seldom live all their lives where they are born. The customer will buy information from you which he could get free, merely because he doesn't know how or doesn't care to write the several letters required. He also believes that the information he buys from you is the "latest dope" available from all sources. The fact that you are offering it for sale convinces him that it is accurate and official.

Suggestions—Make up a list of manufacturing companies in your state. This you can obtain from *Thomas Register*, available at most public libraries. Write to your representatives in your state legislature (not Washington, D.C.) and request information on new industries in the state, tax laws, traffic laws, hunting and fishing information and regulations, housing starts, rental units available, and any other information you feel the job-seeker would find of value or interest. Check supermarket ads and select representative costs for such food items as bread, milk, margarine, hamburger, beef, pork, veal, chicken, vegetables, fruit, and staples such as flour and sugar. Get prices (including tax) on gasoline, cigarettes, and liquor. Compile this information and write a factual report of living conditions and job opportunities in your state and its major cities. Have this printed and also include the list of manufacturers extracted from *Thomas Register* or from your state development commission. This set of fact sheets is your main product and can be sold for between $2 and

$5 and possibly more, depending upon its comprehensive coverage and the national popularity of your state and/or city.

In addition, you can also sell the want-ad section of the Sunday newspaper of one or more of the major cities in your state. A fee of $2 should be charged if sent by regular third class mail. An extra dollar or more should be charged for first class air mail service.

If you have the ability you can also offer a résumé preparation service. The customer supplies the information and you compile this into a one- or two-page printed résumé. You should charge between $25 and $35 for this service, including 100 printed copies, which you mail to your customer. Try to get the full amount in advance. If this does not appear to be feasible, get a deposit of at least $15, or whatever will easily cover the printing cost and represent your protection should the balance due not be forthcoming. To ensure collection of the balance, and with your customer's agreement, you can mail the resumes C.O.D.

If you live in Florida, Arizona, or California you will find that many more people are interested in your employment information service than if you live in Minnesota or Maine, for example. This does not mean that you cannot build a successful business unless you live under perpetual sunshine. (Consider the number of construction jobs on the North Slope in Alaska.) There are attractions in every state which can be as effective in drawing potential customers as a warm climate. Historical interest, natural beauty, educational or recreational facilities, skiing, large lakes or reservoirs, all these can be stressed in your advertising as fringe benefits to living where you do, even if *you* would rather live in Florida or California. Your customer wants to move from where he is and it is your job to cater to this desire while making a profit.

This information service is easy and inexpensive to start and should be considered a possible addition to an existing mail order business. It will mesh well with the sale of research, how-to booklets, remail services, and others. It can also do well alone if you live in the Pacific, Gulf, or Atlantic Coast states, in any industrial state, or in a state which has many tourist attractions.

REMINDER SERVICE

Advantages—A reminder service has very low overhead. Customers will remain with you for years. There is very little work involved, only a few minutes a day. Profits can thus be high. This business can also be operated as a sideline with any other mail order business for greater income. There is little or no competition in this field.

Disadvantages—Your advertising will have to convince the customer that he *needs* your service, that you can provide it at low cost, and that it will relieve him of the necessity for thinking and remembering.

Customer viewpoint—The customer has a lot on his mind and often forgets birthdays, anniversaries, and other important mileposts of life. He welcomes a friendly and timely reminder of these and other important dates. He is willing to pay someone else to do his remembering for him. The more complete the service you offer, the more interest the customer will have and the better your chance for profits.

Suggestions—Set up a tickler file by calendar dates, using 3″ x 5″ file cards. On these cards enter the customer's name and address, the occasions (birthdays, anniversaries, reunions, meetings, etc.) with their dates, any other pertinent information, and place each card in your file under a date approximately 10 to 14 days in advance of the first reminder date.

Have rubber stamps made reading something like: "To remind you of (NAME) (OCCASION) on (DATE) , 19 XYZ Reminder Service, (YOUR ADDRESS). Thank you." Use these to stamp postcards, filling in the blanks. File these with the customer cards. This can be done in your spare time.

Every day, check that date's cards in your file. Remove postcards and place them in your outgoing mail. Date stamp the customer's card with the date of mailing and refile his card 10 to 14 days in advance of the next reminder date.

Charges for this, the main element of your service, should be on an annual basis at a rate of $3 to $5, covering a maximum of ten reminders. Additional reminders should be charged for at 50¢ for one, three for $1 and up to ten for $2.50.

A further service you can offer the customer is handling his greeting card mailings for him. If he supplies the cards and postage you can charge 25¢ to 35¢ for each mailing in addition to your annual fees. If he wishes you to supply the greeting cards, stamp and mail them, you should charge at least a dollar each. This will cover cards costing up to 25¢ retail (which you will buy wholesale at a considerable savings, of course), the stamp, and give you a gross profit of 65¢ to 75¢ each. If your customer insists on more expensive cards—he usually won't—you should charge him additionally the actual retail price of the card plus the $1-per-card fee. Your profit on each will then be almost a dollar.

If you are a poet or writer you can offer to compose unique greetings, inscribing these on blank greeting cards, and charge between $2 and $5 each, depending on the work involved.

If you live in a large city or popular resort area, you can offer additional services. These include making hotel, restaurant, and theater reservations, securing tickets to plays and sporting events, arranging for delivery of flowers, etc. Each reservation you secure should net you $1. You should charge $1 plus 10 percent of the cost of the tickets, flowers, or other merchandise.

BUYING OR SHOPPING SERVICE

Advantages—A buying or shopping service can be operated in your spare time. There is little overhead. Very high profits are possible. There is little or no competition. This service can also be offered as a sideline to other business you do by mail. A week's pay for an hour's time can soon become normal.

Disadvantages—You may in some instances have to be bonded. You may also have to occasionally pack and ship merchandise yourself. You will have to spend much time shopping in the downtown stores. You must live in or very near a large metropolitan area.

Customer viewpoint—The vast majority of your potential customers do not live in New York, Atlanta, New Orleans, Dallas, Chicago, San Francisco, Los Angeles, etc., and they have no way to shop in large city stores. They will be pleased to pay you to do their shopping for them, either on a percentage or fee basis, for there is no other way for them to get what they want.

Suggestions—Offer to shop for whatever the customer wants (as long as it is legal), to stay within the price range he sets, to order the merchandise in his name for shipment C.O.D., and to get the highest possible quality at the lowest cost to him.

You should give the customer the option of paying you either 20 percent of the retail price of the item or on a flat time basis of $5 to $10 per hour for shopping, with a minimum of one hour's charge. If more time is required and the customer is paying you on a time basis, send him a bill for the additional amount due. Most persons will pay, especially if your service and the merchandise are satisfactory.

Since you will be shopping for several customers at a time as your business grows, with a minimum of an hour's charge to each customer or 20 percent per item, you will soon be getting $50, $75, $100 an hour or more for the time you spend shopping.

Most large city stores will pack and ship merchandise C.O.D. to your customer. Some require a deposit. In these instances the customer must send you a deposit for the merchandise, or even its full cost, plus your fee, when he contracts for your services. You should know ahead of time which shops require a deposit, and how much, so you can inform each potential customer of this when he contacts you. It is a good idea to always get a deposit from the customer before you spend time shopping for him.

Since you will be handling money belonging to others you *should* be bonded for your own protection, and stress this fact in your advertising. Bonding guarantees the customer's money; it is a simple matter and bonding companies abound in large cities. A few dollars a year will suffice to bond you for $15,000 which is more than sufficient in most instances.

All your direct mail advertising should state in large type: "Bonded by the ABC Bonding Company." Your classified ads should contain the statement, "Bonded."

OTHER MAIL ORDER OPPORTUNITIES

The product categories and services described in the preceding pages are only a few of those which offer high profits and success in the mail order field. To describe them all, or even to describe in detail those listed in this chapter, would require several books the size of this one.

Practically anything can be sold by mail order if it can be sold at all. Customers with money are waiting to be offered what they want. Look about you for ideas and opportunities. Read advertisements. Visit stores. You may find your product this way if it isn't discussed specifically in this book.

Mail order services are often less trouble (and less work) and usually offer much higher profits than product sales. Services of all kinds are in demand and more customers are willing to pay for services than there are people willing to perform them. While only a few of those with the highest profit potentials are listed here, you will have no difficulty in discovering others. Look for things to do for others which they are unable or unwilling to do for themselves.

Remember—what you *sell* (printed business cards, for example) is rarely what your customer *buys* (convenience, prestige)! Try always to look at your product or service *from the customer's viewpoint*. If you will find out what the *customer* wants and offer it to him, he will pay you handsomely and willingly.

LOCATING SUPPLIERS

So you've selected a product to sell that seems to meet the criteria of a good mail order item. Now where do you find a place to buy it from or manufacture it so you can sell it? Of course, if you're selling rough stones that you have collected yourself or an employment information service, you don't have to find a supplier—you "manufacture" the product yourself. But other kinds of products will need a supplier.

You will come across many suppliers in your search for a product. As mentioned in the previous chapter, when you see products advertised that you may be interested in selling, write to the manufacturer or outlet and get a sample. That manufacturer is a possible supplier. At your public library look in *Thomas Register* under the name of your chosen product, and write down the names of companies who manufacture your product. These companies are also potential suppliers.

Don't overlook any possible source for a product. A classified ad placed in the "Wanted to Buy" column in your local newspaper or in a nearby large city newspaper may reveal a local inventor, manufacturer, or writer who has or can produce the ideal product for you to sell.

Write to each possible supplier on your list to get quotes on prices and shipping details. Or better yet, send each supplier a request for quotation (RFQ). This special form is described in chapter 10. Using an RFQ can save you money, because it can sometimes get a better price than the ones listed in the manufacturers' advertisements and catalogs. Fill in your RFQs, describing what you want to buy, and mail them to each supplier on your list. Each company will return it to you listing the price they will sell at and their terms of payment. Assuming several suppliers can give you equal quality goods, you will usually choose the supplier who offers the best price. (RFQs, determining the lowest bid, and ordering procedures are discussed in more detail in chapter 10.)

Naming Your Price and Your Company

If you are selling merchandise direct from classified ads, you will need to know your selling price before you prepare and place the ad. But if your classified ads are to draw customers' inquiries prior to their placing an order (the type of operation this book focuses on), then you don't need to print the price in the classified. However, you *will* need to determine the price before you prepare and print the follow-up mailing materials.

Your company name and address is an important consideration, too. It must have sales appeal and be concise enough so it does not take up a lot of space in your classified ads—each letter can cost you money.

MAIL ORDER PRICING

Pricing of mail order products and services differs considerably from the pricing of merchandise in the retail store. Almost never is selling price in mail order determined by a formula based upon a percentage mark-up over cost to include overhead and profit. Most mail order prices are adjusted to be as close as possible to the maximum amount the greatest number of customers are willing to pay, without any regard to actual cost. In other words, the mail order price is optimized from a psychological standpoint. Thus, an item which costs you 50¢ may sell for anything from about $2 to $10, depending upon many things, the least of which is how much it cost you.

In pricing merchandise *in the retail store for over-the-counter sales*, the cost to the customer includes all of the following:

1. Retailer's cost, overhead, and profit.
2. Dealer's cost, overhead, and profit.

3. Distributor's cost, overhead, and profit.
4. Wholesaler's cost, overhead, and profit.
5. Manufacturer's cost, overhead and profit.

The overhead in each case includes taxes, wages and salaries, rent, utilities, depreciation, forms and files, transportation, insurance, and other costs. Because the product changes hands so many times between the original manufacturer and the eventual consumer, and *overhead and profit* is added to its cost each time it changes hands, you can easily realize that an item costing but a few cents to manufacture will probably cost several dollars by the time the consumer buys it at retail.

In mail order most of these middlemen are eliminated from the chain extending between the manufacturer and the eventual user. You will either be the manufacturer or the wholesaler in every case, thus cutting out at least three other middlemen and the cost of their overhead and profits. This gives you considerable flexibility in determining your selling price and assures you a profit which can be quite large in comparison to the profit any one company can earn on a similar item merchandised through normal retail channels.

PRICE ADVANTAGE IN MAIL ORDER

Naturally you want to set a price which will bring in the most income. *This does not necessarily mean the most sales.* You must strike a balance between sales volume and profits. You must always keep your overhead in mind when determining selling prices, but only to the extent that your income will pay not only all your costs but also show a good net profit.

Since you will probably be starting your business at home rather than in separate, rented facilities, your real overhead expenses can be quite low. Facilities costs—rent, utilities (electricity, gas, water, sewer and garbage charges, telephone bills, etc.)—for your home are no larger after you start in business than they were before. In fact, that portion of normal home expenses assignable to your business are deductible against business income and actually result in a profit to you rather than an expense.

Your actual out-of-pocket overhead expenses include advertising, postage, printing, product costs, and the cost of office equipment, all of which are deductible expenses. All except capital equipment costs are deductible in the year in which they were incurred, while the cost of capital equipment (equipment expected to have a normal life span in excess of one year) is recovered over a period of years through deductions for depreciation. Thus, except for higher costs for postage and printing, these portions of your overhead expenses are similar to those of any *one* of the middlemen in the normal retail merchandising chain. The fact that most of these middlemen have extra facilities costs and must also pay wages and salaries more than balances out your increased costs for postage and printing. Therefore, the costs of overhead and profit in the retail merchandising chain represent a buffer area within which you can establish your selling price. This allows you a much greater profit potential even though your selling price may be lower than that of comparable items sold through retail stores.

THE CUSTOMER'S VIEWPOINT

The customer expects two things from a mail order company. First, he expects a somewhat lower price than he might have to pay for a similar item locally. Second, he expects a bonus in uniqueness, quality, flexibility, something not obtainable by him locally. It is up to you to give him what he expects.

The public has long been conditioned through the catalogs of the giant mail order department stores to expect a lower (but not much lower) price on items ordered by mail. This lower price represents to the customer a bonus to repay him for his patience in waiting a few days to two weeks between the time he recognizes his want (by mailing his order) and the time it is satisfied (when he receives his order in the mail).

You have a large buffer between your cost-plus-overhead and the normal retail selling price of a similar item, so you will have no difficulty in giving the customer the somewhat lower price he expects. But you must be careful not to make your price too much lower, or else the customer will suspect that your offer is shoddy and lacking in quality. You should adjust your selling price with this in mind and quietly pocket the extra profits.

The customer's second requirement of uniqueness and quality may be more difficult to provide. Yet you must do so to have a successful, growing, and profitable business. It is no use to attempt to sell him something he can buy locally for a little more money. He'll pay the difference for the convenience of getting what he wants when he wants it, without waiting for a mail delivery. You must offer him something he cannot obtain locally at any price, although it can be *similar* to items which may be available to him from other sources.

What you offer him—at a price somewhat lower than similar items— must satisfy some of the desires discussed in chapter 1. It must do this better than similar items; in other words it must be unique or at least different in a manner which the customer will consider better and therefore desirable. Suggestions for suitable mail order products and services are given in chapter 3. Within these and similar categories, search out the unique, the better, the different, upon which to establish your business.

WHAT YOU CAN CHARGE

Retail businesses can take advantage of effective pricing in odd amounts like $1.98, $3.98, $4.95, $9.99, etc. The mail order business cannot because some of your customers will send cash instead of a check or money order. He finds it easy to clip a $5 bill to his order and slip it into your return envelope. He will not even attempt to put in four $1 bills and 95¢ in change; nor will he usually send you $5 if your price is $4.95. To the average person, $4.95 *seems* like only a little over $4.00, much less than $5.00, despite the fact of only a 5¢ difference. This quirk of human nature is the reason behind so many items being offered for sale in stores at odd prices. Even new and used automobiles are priced this way. This is a very effective method of pricing at a retail level where buyer and seller meet personally. Unfortunately, it cannot usually be used for selling by mail order.

Mail order goods are most often priced in whole dollar amounts. The public will usually purchase directly from a classified ad items offered for $1, $2, up to approximately $5, but seldom if the price is higher. Most such orders will contain dollar bills. However, the costs of advertising and particularly postage make it almost impossible to make a profit on an item selling for $1, even if you get it free. Two dollars is about the minimum for anything sold by mail as a single product, though lower-priced goods can be sold profitably if each order is for several items and the total order is for a reasonable dollar value.

Above approximately $5 you should not attempt to make sales directly from your classified ad. Instead, use your ad to get inquiries and follow them up with direct mail sales messages. There will be little sales resistance *based on price alone* for items selling for $10 or less. Above this amount the number of orders drops off sharply and rarely will a more expensive item alone support a beginning operation. As was discussed in chapter 1, the customer will gamble a relatively small amount. Rarely will he risk more than $10 unless he is dealing with one of the giant mail order companies who have been in business for many years and with whose advertising and products he has become familiar.

Keep your price as high as is practicable but below $10 if at all possible. Watch your overhead expenses. Buy the products you sell at the lowest prices. Take advantage of all discounts and quantity price breaks. Do these things and it will be almost impossible not to make money.

YOUR COMPANY NAME AND ADDRESS

There are two primary reasons why you should give almost as much attention to your company name and address as to the sales copy in your advertising:

1. You pay for each separate word and figure group in your name and address. Keep it short.
2. Your company name should be distinctive, yet not so exclusive that you could not sell other products or services under the same name when you expand.

Considering No. 1 above, you probably should rent a post office box for your business mail (it's tax deductible) unless your street address contains only two word groups: *201 Broadway* costs the same as *Box 12345*. But *375 Columbus Circle* costs more since it contains three word groups. If you have a rural address, *Route 2* for instance, you should also rent a box, even though the cost of including your address in the ad is the same.

The reader willingly deludes himself that every company which advertises with a box number and most with a street address is a thriving business with its own large, new building, even though he really knows better. But a rural route address makes him think of Farmer Brown rather than a business concern. There is nothing to be gained by shattering the reader's vision of you. Allow him to dream on. Rent a box at the post office.

The problem inherent in No. 2 above is more complex. Many a person wishes to use his own name as a company name, while others will not do this for their own reasons. Either choice can be acceptable.

Extremely common names (Smith, Jones, Brown), unusual or hard to pronounce names (Chomondeley, Worcestershire), and foreign-sounding names (Leiberhund, Dorndorffer, Vicompte) are questionable choices as company names. Selection must remain a personal choice, however. Two advantages in using your own name as a company name are individuality in some instances, and usually your name does not indicate any specific product or service.

If you choose a company name, including a word similar to *automotive, sporting,* or *recreation,* you limit your sales to products and services within the indicated categories. It would seem incongruous for an auto accessory company to offer toys or baby clothes for sale.

Since most of you are just starting out in mail order, a company name which is attractive, both in type and to the ear, should be chosen. Preferably it should not indicate a type of product or service. It should be so chosen that you could include many different types of products and services. Some typical examples are given below.

Associated Enterprises	Acme Services
American Products	Product Sales
Sales Associates	Columbia Sales
Universal Sales	Import Sales
United Distributors	Wholesale Products
Official Sales	Apex Distributors

New Product Sales	Ultimate Services
Products Unlimited	Services Unlimited
New Idea Sales	Sunshine Services
Sun Coast Products	Gold Coast Sales
Costal Services	Woodlawn Products
Royal Sales	Enterprises Unlimited

Some of the names listed are probably being used today and no claim to originality is made. It will be preferable if you do not use any of the exact company names given here but instead create your own, using these as a guide.

The words *sales, services,* and *products* in these company names are interchangeable. If you deal in both products and services, or think you might do so as your business expands, don't use either of these terms. Stick to something neutral like *enterprises* or *associates* or other nondefinitive catch-all words.

Keep your company name short to keep the cost of insertion down in those publications which charge by the word and not by the line. In both name and address, strive for brevity as illustrated in the following imaginary example. It contains only six "words" but is complete including zip code.

ACME, Box 11738, Dover, DE 19901

ZIP CODE AND STATE ABBREVIATIONS

Be sure to include your zip code with your address in all advertising matter. Some periodicals do not charge for this; some do. Including your zip code is worthwhile in view of the poor handwriting that many people have, since the numerals can often be read by the post office although the rest of the address may be undecipherable. Mail which otherwise might be sent to the dead letter office may still be delivered to you if the zip code and either the name or address are readable. *Every letter addressed to you is either an inquiry or an order. Be sure you get them.*

Two-letter abbreviations of the names of the states were approved by the U.S. Postal Service in 1963. These are always to be printed in block capital letters and are intended, along with the zip code, for eventual automation in mail handling. Become familiar with these abbreviations. Use them in your ads and on your letters.

Alabama	AL	California	CA
Alaska	AK	Colorado	CO
Arizona	AZ	Connecticut	CT
Arkansas	AR	Delaware	DE

Dist. of Columbia	DC	New Jersey	NJ
Florida	FL	New Mexico	NM
Georgia	GA	New York	NY
Guam	GU	North Carolina	NC
Hawaii	HI	North Dakota	ND
Idaho	ID	Ohio	OH
Illinois	IL	Oklahoma	OK
Indiana	IN	Oregon	OR
Iowa	IA	Pennsylvania	PA
Kansas	KS	Puerto Rico	PR
Kentucky	KY	Rhode Island	RI
Louisiana	LA	South Carolina	SC
Maine	ME	South Dakota	DS
Maryland	MD	Tennessee	TN
Massachusetts	MA	Texas	TX
Michigan	MI	Utah	UT
Minnesota	MN	Vermont	VT
Mississippi	MS	Virginia	VA
Missouri	MO	Virgin Islands	VI
Montana	MT	Washington	WA
Nebraska	NE	West Virginia	WV
Nevada	NV	Wisconsin	WI
New Hampshire	NH	Wyoming	WY

YOUR LEGAL RESPONSIBILITIES

The most recent federal laws concerning mail order merchandising are intended to protect the customer from unscrupulous dealers. Since the penalties for breaking these laws can be great, it is important that you know exactly what you can and cannot do in dealing with your customers. However, laws are subject to change, so before you place your first ad, you should write to the Federal Trade Commission, Washington, DC 20580 and ask for their folder dealing with mail order regulations.

As for tax laws, and any state and local laws regarding licensing, your local IRS office and your county clerk's office are your best sources of information. At first, if you are just starting up a one-man operation, your income can be reported as ordinary income on your yearly tax returns, and you can take appropriate business deductions. If you are on record as "self-employed," however, you will have to file quarterly estimations of income and pay the estimated income and FICA (Social Security) taxes in quarterly installments.

5

Classifieds Don't Cost–They Pay

GETTING THE ATTENTION OF THE PAYING CUSTOMER

No matter how marvelous your product, how quick your service, or how low your prices, your customers cannot buy unless you tell them about it. Since you cannot tell them in person, you will have to advertise.

You must place your message where the potential customer will see it. You must attract his attention. You must get and hold his interest. You must convince him that you have just what he needs right now. Make him aware that such a need exists. You must get him to take the trouble of writing and mailing a postcard or letter to you, possibly including money.

Advertising presents your sales proposition to potential customers. *It is your salesman.* In fact, because it is distributed so widely, it represents thousands of salesmen for your product or service. These salesmen go into the homes and offices of your potential customers with your message. Along with them come hundreds of other salesmen—other advertisements—all competing for the customer's money, all offering a silent but well-thought-out sales presentation.

The customer is exposed to hundreds of newspaper and magazine ads; each day he sees billboards, car cards, posters, window signs, and point-of-sale ads. His ears and eyes are assaulted with innumerable commercials on radio and television programs. He tends to become partially deaf and blind to most advertising messages and will "turn off" most messages because the volume is overwhelming.

Classified ads are the ones you will be using to find your customer and attract him with your offer, and it is these ads which are considered here.

Once he has replied to your classified ad, you have the opportunity to present your proposition in detail with direct mail advertising (leaflets, broadsides, pamphlets, etc.) which do not have immediate competition. These materials are discussed in chapter 7.

The first and most important job your classified ad must do is to *get the customer's attention*. All of the competing ads are also trying to do the same thing. Getting the customer's attention is vital. No matter how wonderful your offer, *if the customer doesn't read it he cannot buy*, and your "salesman" is ineffective. The money he has cost you (the price you paid for your ad to be printed) is wasted.

As the reader's eye skims over the page containing your ad, you will have only a split second to catch his eye, halt it, and get his attention. *All* other ads on the same page as yours compete for the reader's attention. You have no way of knowing ahead of time what methods other advertisers will use, yet you will have to try to beat them at their own game. *You may not know the players but you must know the rules*.

There is almost no opportunity for distinctive visual impact as an attention-getter in a normal classified ad. Publishers rarely allow a choice of typeface and never any artwork. (Display classifieds—the ones with pictures—are quite different, and quite expensive.) They often permit, at additional cost, heavier type or all block capital letters or both. They always allow a headline, if you wish one, at a slight additional cost. Since these are the only variables over which you have any control in a classified ad, here is where you will gain or lose the reader.

Part of the attention-getting job is already done for you automatically by the method of classification. Only those readers who might be interested in your offer will be attracted to your ad. This prescreening reduces the amount of competition your ad faces while increasing its effect. No one who might be interested in boating accessories, for instance, will look for such ads in a column classified "Stamps and Coins."

WHAT ADVERTISING MUST ACCOMPLISH

For an advertisement to be successful it must produce sales. It must produce enough sales to cover its cost and that of overhead. It must return the cost of the product or service and your time. It must cover shipping costs, and add enough more to provide an acceptable profit for you. If your advertisements do not do this reasonably consistently, you will not long remain in business. Your advertising, then, is even more critically important than the service or product you sell. Without successful advertising you have no customers. Without customers you have no business and no income.

There are four things every successful advertisement *must* achieve.

They will be easy to remember if you think of Verdi's opera *Aida*. The letters *AIDA* are the initial letters of the words which describe every successful ad's results:

A   *Attention.* Your ad must get the reader's attention before anything else can be accomplished.

I   *Interest.* After you have the reader's attention you must get and *keep* his interest.

D   *Determination.* Your ad must give the reader the determination that he wants what you have to offer.

A   *Action.* The reader must be spurred to act, to send in an order or a request for more information.

Thus your ad must catch the reader's eye and make him interested enough to read it further to find out more about your offer. Immediately it must disclose the advantages your offer has over your competitors. You must then prove these to the reader. He must be persuaded to recognize and believe these advantages. Finally, your ad must *ask for action* and make it as easy as possible for the reader to do whatever it is you require of him.

ANALYZING YOUR PRODUCT'S APPEAL

Take a close look at whatever product or service you are trying to sell. Make a list with pencil and paper of everything you can find out about it, *good and bad*. Often the same point will be found in both the "good" and "bad" categories. So-called bad points can usually be presented, if necessary, in such a way that they become good selling points.

List all types of people whom you think might buy what you have to sell. Decide what magazines or newspapers they probably read. At the beginning you probably will not wish and cannot afford to run classified ads in every likely magazine under each appropriate classification. However, get as much of this information about your product or service on paper as you can. You will have a continuing need for it.

In determining which magazines your potential customers read, study the information in *Writer's Market*. Your public library should have a copy. You may also purchase a copy from *Writer's Digest*, 9933 Alliance Road, Cincinnati, OH 45242. *Writer's Market* is published annually. The 1979 edition costs $14.50. Many of the thousands of magazines listed state who their readership is, often by sex, age group, religion, education, or other means. You can also determine what interests their readers by noting what the editor has to say regarding the kind of stories and articles published. This book represents probably the best comprehensive and current source of readership information generally available.

You can also gain insight into the type of person who reads various magazines by reading both the advertising and editorial contents of many magazines. Public libraries subscribe to numerous magazines, and you probably have several at home. If you are on especially good terms with your local news dealer, he may allow you to browse through the magazines on his stand.

To serve as an example, assume that you are selling this book by mail order and that it is the only product you have to offer. (This same assumption will be used in the rest of this book when considering advertising practices and materials. These practices and materials can readily be adapted to whatever *you* are selling.)

Now make your lists, keeping in mind the customer traits given in chapter 1.

Good Points
1. Valuable information on how to operate a profitable business.
2. Easy to understand by anyone with a limited education.
3. Requires no specialized knowledge.
4. Offers opportunity for high income.
5. Offers security.
6. Offers independence.
7. Unnecessary to meet individual customers; no direct selling.
8. Offers prestige in the community.
9. Enables gaining recognition as a business person.
10. Price is low compared to opportunity offered.
11. Will not go out of date.
12. Well printed and bound, with clear illustrations.
13. Complete. Nothing else needed to know to make good money.
14. Nothing else available is as comprehensive and practical.
15. Appeals to people bored with current jobs.
16. Appeals to married women needing income.
17. Requires very limited investment. Can be started on a shoe-string.
18. Requires little room. Can be started at home.
19. Shows ambition and superior ability.
20. Appeals to men and women of all ages.

This list of good points is far from complete. There are many more which you could add. However, those listed include the most important and are sufficient examples. Now, list the bad points.

Bad Points
1. No repeat sales.
2. Costs more than $5; probably cannot be sold directly from classified ad.

3. Requires packaging before shipment.
4. Requires space for inventory.
5. Might receive competition if a similar book is later written by another.

Again, this list of "bad points" is probably incomplete, although the author has honestly tried to think of all of them. Now, let's first consider these bad points.

Take the first bad point, no repeat sales. This results from a product that will not go out of date (good point No. 11) and is complete, nothing else needed to know to make good money (good point No. 13). So bad point No. 1 is really a good point *from the customer's point of view*.

Bad point No. 2 concerns price. True, an item costing more than $5 may be somewhat difficult to sell directly from an ad. It is much more easily sold by follow-up direct mail advertising, material you mail to the readers who reply to your ad. However, its price is also a valuable selling point (see good points no. 10, 11, 13, and 14. Most of the others also support this contention.)

Bad points No. 3 and 4 are common to all merchandise which you must handle directly. This, however, *has no effect on the customer* who couldn't care less about your personal problems. Remember to look carefully at your product *from the customer's viewpoint*.

Bad point No. 5 is the automatic result of the appearance of any worthwhile product. It will be imitated. Nothing can be done about it except that you must strive to have the best product when competition appears. Being first on the market, long before the competition, is a terrific advantage. If you're first, many persons will have seen your ads by the time the competition arrives, and though they may not yet be your customers, they may in the future.

CHOOSING THE BEST CLASSIFICATION

Look over the list of good points applicable to this book and consider the person to whom each should appeal. Summarize these and you will probably end up by deciding the product should appeal to men and women of all ages who need or want more money, independence, security, the admiration and respect of others; who are not at present as successful as they wish and are dissatisfied with what they are doing; who probably do not have much formal education; who feel that, given an opportunity to show what they can do, would soon prove their abilities; who have some but not a lot of money saved; who have the ambition to be successful and the ability to get there.

This is a fairly close analysis of the person you want to reach with your classified ads. To narrow the choice down to a reasonable number, look over each classification which might apply:

1. Of Interest to Women
2. Of Interest to Men
3. Business Opportunities
4. Instructions, Information
5. Books, Periodicals
6. Employment Information
7. Money-Making Opportunities
8. Help Wanted—Male and Female
9. Mail Order Opportunities

The above list, admittedly incomplete, lists the most obvious classifications. The pros and cons of each are considered in the following paragraphs.

1. Of Interest to Women. This classification can be safely ignored. Most of your customers will be men. Women read other classifications, too.

2. Of Interest to Men. This, too, is too general. Your ad would be lost in the midst of others for many unrelated items.

3. Business Opportunities. This is a possibility. Most ads in this classification are placed by manufacturers looking for salesmen, however, and so it is not the best choice.

4. Instructions, Information. This is good. This book could well be advertised under this classification and sold successfully.

5. Books, Periodicals. A possibility, but not as good as No. 4.

6. Employment Information. A possibility, but most ads in this classification offer job information. You would reach only a portion of your potential customers.

7. Money-Making Opportunities. A good possibility. *This is what the customer is really buying—a chance to make money.*

8. Help Wanted—Male and Female. Not selective enough. Readers of these ads are looking for work to do, not businesses to start.

9. Mail Order Opportunities. The best of those given. Your ad will reach all readers who are already interested in mail order. While other ads will compete with yours, very likely all will be read, or partly read.

Your obvious choice, if this book were your product, is No. 9. Runners up are No. 7, 4, and 5, in that order.

Some magazines and newspapers may not normally have the particular classification you want for your ad. Some will insist that you use the closest classification they have. Others, however, will insert the classification heading you desire and run your ad under it. If you can arrange this you will gain much better results since your ad will probably be the only one under this particular classification. You not only have the space you paid for, but also an extra quarter-inch or so immediately above, containing the classification in big, black, bold letters. This will help considerably in attracting readers to your offer.

In newspapers, particularly, you might consider the classifications "Personals," "Business Personals," and "Miscellaneous." While not specifically applicable (except "Business Personals") these classifications enjoy widespread readership. However, they do not screen the readers to attract those you really want to reach while excluding the rest. Your ad will be competing for the reader's attention among many other advertisements.

THE ALL-IMPORTANT HEADLINE

The classification you run your ad under prescreens readers, and if you have selected the best one (or several) your ad will be exposed primarily to only interested persons. You will have competition from nearby ads, however, and you must direct the reader's attention to yours. Use a headline to accomplish this. Since others will also use block capital letters and heavy type, the only way to make your ad stand out is with the words you use.

The first ten words are more important than the next ten thousand!

Some of these first ten words will be in your headline. They must be very carefully chosen so they will cause the reader's eye to stop when it reaches your ad. You have only a second, more or less, to accomplish this feat, so *your headline must have a basic emotional appeal.* Use words which, even at a glance, penetrate the reader's subconscious and cause him to stop and consider.

There are numerous words you can use in your headline to get the reader's attention. Examples of these are given below. As you read them, note how many grab your own interest and make you curious as to what the missing words in each partial headline might be.

THE SECRET OF . . .	REVEALED . . .
HOW I . . .	PROFITS FOR YOU . . .
SAVE . . .	DO WONDERS WITH . . .
WHY . . .	DID YOU SEE . . . ?
NO MORE . . .	MAKE THIS TEST . . .
WHO ELSE WANTS . . .	WHERE YOU CAN . . .
DON'T LET . . .	HOW TO . . .
DOES YOUR . . . ?	NOW YOU CAN . . .
NAME YOUR . . .	MISTAKES THAT COST . . .
DISCOVER . . .	ADVICE TO . . . BY . . .

HOW MUCH . . .
WHICH . . .
NEW DISCOVERY . . .
WE'LL HELP YOU . . .
HOW YOU CAN . . .
. . . PROVES . . .
273 WAYS TO . . .
THROW AWAY YOUR . . .
IMAGINE ME . . .
DID YOU HEAR . . . ?
ANNOUNCING . . .
WHERE TO . . .
A QUICK WAY . . .
49 REASONS WHY . . .
ARE THEY . . . ?
ARE YOU . . . ?
OWN YOUR OWN . . .

TAKE . . .
FREE! SECRETS . . .
FREE BOOK . . .
IS PROSPERITY WORTH
   $5.75 . . .
WHAT YOU SHOULD
   KNOW ABOUT . . .
FOR THE (PERSON)
   WHO . . .
AN EASY WAY . . .
SUPPOSE . . .
ARE WE . . . ?
MONEY-SAVING . . .
NOW! YOU CAN . . .
CHOOSE . . .
BARGAIN . . .
SALE PRICED . . .

When using figures, be specific. Odd numbers have more impact than even amounts: 273 seems more accurate than 300 or nearly 300: $5.75 is better than $5.00 or $6.00.

Using the examples given, or your own ideas, write several headlines for your ad. Go back over the list of good points (selling ideas and emotional appeals). If you are selling this book as a mail order product, you might write some headlines like these:

1. NAME YOUR OWN INCOME
2. BE YOUR OWN BOSS
3. OWN YOUR OWN BUSINESS
4. YOUR EASY MONEY BUSINESS
5. DO YOU WANT MORE MONEY?
6. INCOME AND SECURITY FOR YOU
7. SUCCESS THE EASY WAY
8. IS PROSPERITY WORTH $0.00 TO YOU?
9. WHO ELSE WANTS MORE MONEY?
10. REVEALED! MAIL ORDER SUCCESS SECRETS
11. HOW MUCH INCOME DO YOU WANT?

Most of the above are good headlines and many more could be written which may be equally effective. Notice that *they all tell the customer what he can have*. They all answer the question "What's in it for me?" in varying ways. All appeal to man's basic instincts. All are truthful.

Of all of the above list, No. 2 and 3 are trite. They have been used so often they no longer have original appeal. Of the remainder, the author feels that No. 1 has the broadest appeal, with No. 9 and 6 the runners-up. However, this is a personal opinion. Yours may be better. After all, it is *your* business which concerns *you!*

Do not tell all in your headline, even if this is possible. Your headline should interest, pique curiosity, tease the reader into reading your ad. Save your big guns for your direct mail follow-up advertising where you have all the space you need and which your customer can read at leisure. Your classified ad should be constructed to get your customer to reply to you by mail, requesting additional information, unless you are selling something direct from your ad for less than about $5. Even if your price is under $5, offering something FREE (information), and getting inquiries will result in greater sales volume and higher profits than will sales direct from your classified ad. It also makes it easier for you to secure repeat business.

HOLDING THE READER'S INTEREST

It is much easier to get the reader's interest than to hold it!

Your headline has caught the reader's eye, his attention, has made him curious to know more. The job the body copy (the rest of your ad, after the headline) must do first is to hold his interest and then to generate enthusiasm. This is not simple. Your choice of words remains very important.

In a classified ad you usually have space for only a limited number of words. Limited space need not restrict the selling impact of your ad, however. In fact, the size of the ad and even the size of the headline are of little importance. As an example, an ad containing a photograph often has a headline in large black type. Just beneath the photograph will be a short line of very small, light type called a *cut line* which gives picture credits or other explanation of the picture. *The cut line is read more often than the headline!* No one can tell you why your customer shows this illogical response. He is not always logical and often seems to be unpredictable.

Long classified ads will often not be read through. Too, the cost per word or per line of classified ads in those publications which produce the most sales is so high that your advertising expenses rise rapidly with large ads.

Words which don't help, hurt!

Remember that statement. It is all too true. Whether your ad contains 15, 25, or 40 words, each costs you money and each must be made to work as hard as possible. A word which contributes nothing only wastes money. It actually detracts from the effectiveness of your message. Be ruthless in cutting out words which do no work. A short ad in which every word works hard will earn more money for you than a longer ad containing lazy words. Hard, tight writing costs less in advertising dollars.

The *average* reader has a surprisingly limited vocabulary, usually between 3000 and 5000 words. Because of this you must adjust your advertising vocabulary to match his. Keep big, fancy words out of your ads, even if they express your meaning aptly and accurately. The reader may not understand the nuances of the word and this may alienate him. At best, it makes it difficult for him to read and understand your message. If you don't make everything as easy as possible for the reader to grasp your meaning he will be lost as a potential customer.

To write the body copy, refer to your list of good and bad points and your analysis of the most likely customer. Pick out some of the selling points which have emotional appeal to your customer and write several ads. *Make every word work for you.* Cut your ad down to the fewest *simple,* effective words which contain the best and most complete appeal to the reader.

Below is a series of classified ads using this book as an example. Note how the wording changes as the ad copy is tightened to make it shorter, yet the final ad has terrific punch. These ads are constructed according to the AIDA formula (attention, interest, determination, action) explained at the beginning of this chapter.

Do these ads get your attention, hold your interest, give you determination to do something about your circumstances, and ask for action on your part? Is the final ad better than the first one?

NAME YOUR OWN INCOME
Security for you. Be your own boss. Start small, grow big fast. No ceiling on income. No selling. Money, orders in your mail every day. Mail order secrets revealed. All you need to know in new book. Free details. No obligation ever. Guaranteed. Write today.

NAME YOUR OWN INCOME
No selling. Work home. Start today, grow big fast. Orders, money arrive daily. Big profits. Guaranteed. New book tells how. Complete. Details free. Write.

NAME YOUR OWN INCOME
No selling. Work home. Guaranteed. Profits daily. Grow big fast. New book reveals secrets, tells how. Free details. Write now.

The first ad contains 49 words. Compare it with the final ad which contains only 24 words. Words have been reduced by more than half, yet the ad contains *all* the information given in the first version. *Every word is now working hard!*

Look at the final version of the ad. *Of the 24 words it contains, 16 have one syllable and only 7 have two.* The single three-syllable word, *guaranteed,* is familiar to everyone. All these words are simple and familiar. All will be easily understood, even by children in elementary school and certainly by the average reader with a 3000 to 5000 word vocabulary. This does not mean that an occasional multisyllable word may never be used or that only one- and two-syllable words should always be used. But short, simple words are best, and great care must be used in choosing *all* words, regardless of length or the number of syllables they contain.

EFFECTIVE (AND ETHICAL) COPY

Look again at the final version of the classified ad above. Consider the headline. It screams for attention and promises that anyone can earn as much money as he wishes. By *implication* it also promises security, prestige, admiration, respect, good food, big cars, a big house, vacations, all that money can buy. *Only four words do all this!* Those four words were chosen very carefully as, of course, were the remaining twenty words included in the final version.

As stressed earlier, the first ten words are more important than the next ten thousand. Consider the first ten words in the body copy of the ad and *what they say as well as what they imply to the reader.* These words are "No Selling. Work home. Guaranteed. Profits daily. Grow big fast."

First, they appeal to man's innate laziness by telling him he does not have to do any selling. Most people hate the thought of meeting someone face-to-face and trying to sell him something. Selling is work, and the reader really doesn't want to be forced to work.

These words further appeal by telling the reader he doesn't have to leave home to gain all the benefits suggested in the headline. From this he infers, as the words imply, that he can be his own boss, set his own hours, pretty much do as he pleases. In other words, he can have security and independence.

By *guaranteed* is meant—truthfully—that the book is being offered on a money-back-if-not-satisfied basis and that the headline and the first four words of body copy are true as well, which of course they are.

The reader, however, will usually infer that success is what is guaranteed, and he tends to couple *Guaranteed* with the phrases which follow—*Profits daily* and *Grow big fast*—although a period has been inserted after the word *Guaranteed* to make it stand alone.

No ad can guarantee success, profits, or growth, of course, and this ad *has not done so.* Legally it could not, and strictly from a legal standpoint it has actually guaranteed nothing! The word "guaranteed" standing alone has no legal applicability. While you can assume that the reader will make the inferences stated above because you have analyzed what will appeal to him and how he will react to certain words and phrases, this does not mean that your ad is not ethical.

Your job is not so much to sell the reader as it is to cause him to sell himself.

Since you only want the reader to request additional information and are not asking him in the ad to send money, the ad represents ethical advertising practice. It is an example of psychology applied to secure a mutually advantageous result.

The next phrase, *Profits daily*, tells the reader that money will arrive in every mail delivery, and implies that money and orders will come together. They will—*if he establishes his business and operates it as instructed* in this book, which you will offer for sale in follow-up advertising sent to him when he replies to your classified ad. This phrase reinforces the promise in the headline and implies the security of a continued income. It also leads into the next phrase and reinforces it as well.

The final three words of the important first ten tell the reader he *can*, and implies that he *will*, increase his income rapidly.

The words *big* and *fast* are abstract words not having simple, well-understood definitions. How big is "big?" How fast is "fast"? The reader supplies his own definitions to these words. *Big* may mean $1000 to an unemployed person, $10,000 to someone else, and $1 million to another. *Fast* also depends upon the reader's own definitions: a month, a year, five years? You gain a lot from such hard-working words because *they mean whatever the reader wants them to mean*. Thus, *such words automatically appeal to all readers*. This is quite ethical and is extremely effective advertising.

GETTING THE READER TO ACT

The headline has attracted the reader's attention. The first ten words of body copy in the ad have not only held his interest, they have given him the desire and, hopefully, the determination that *he* can do something about his present circumstances. The next phrase in the ad, *New book reveals secrets, tells how*, contains only six short words. These six words reinforce his determination by telling him he can get the information he needs and now wants to fulfill the promise of the headline. First, it tells him that all he needs to know is contained in a book, and that the book is new. He knows from experience that books seldom cost much more than $10. Therefore he knows he will not be asked to risk much money. The fact that the book is new implies that he can get in on the ground floor, giving him an advantage over others.

The words *reveals secrets* tells him that the book will tell him trade secrets or short-cut methods never before available from a single source (which it does). He probably infers that some deep, dark, magic formula for success is contained in the book.

Secrets is another valuable abstract word to which most readers will apply their own definitions. Again, this is ethical advertising and truthful, though there is no magic involved, merely plain common sense and applied psychology. The "secrets" are not widely known and are not available in any other single publication to the best of this author's knowledge and belief, and the methods explained in this book are proven in practice. Because many of the things disclosed in this book are known only to a few psychologists and advertising and merchandising men and women, they actually are trade secrets.

The last two words of this phrase, *tells how*, tells the reader that all he needs to know to enable him to fulfill the promise of the headline are in this one new book. True. General and specific instructions for every phase of the mail order business are made clear and explained in detail. *This is the convincer, the final punch to crystallize the reader's determination to act.*

Consider how much you have accomplished with only six words, words which weren't even included in the first ten!

The last four words in the ad, *Free details. Write now,* tell the reader that you will provide answers to the many questions in his mind and tell him all about the book, and that this will be done absolutely free and at no cost nor obligation to him.

He is then told, or asked, *write now.* This tells him that a simple postcard or letter to you will bring him free information immediately. It also stresses that the reader should act *now,* implying that later may be too late and strongly reinforcing the idea that the longer he delays the more he is losing, that quick action means he will be able to "name his own income" that much sooner.

It has taken approximately 1300 words in this chapter just to describe how a 24-word classified ad can affect the average reader. Yet a 1300-word advertisement would hardly result in more than a very few replies; most persons would not read it. But the same information reduced to 24 hard-working words will load your mail box. *It isn't what you know, it's how you say it.*

Your classified ad is not complete until your company name and address are included at the end of your advertising message. As discussed in chapter 4, the name of your company and its address should be worded carefully so it is attractive, impressive, yet brief enough to take full advantage of your classified ad space. A post office box number is recommended. Use the two-letter state code, and *always* include your zip code.

6 Periodicals— Choosing and Using Them

Periodicals are newspapers and magazines. They are the showcase in which you will present your classified ad. Each one has its audience and there is considerable overlap in readership between magazines and newspapers. Newspaper readers read magazines and vice versa. Which one you use, when and how often, depends mainly on the product or service you are selling.

NEWSPAPER ADVERTISING

There are three distinct types of newspapers, each of which reaches a different audience: large metropolitan daily newspapers, other daily newspapers, and weekly newspapers. Large metropolitan dailies are read primarily by workers and executives. Not too many middle-income people live in the large cities, but some subscribe to these metropolitan papers though they live in the suburbs. This is particularly true of Sunday editions.

The remaining daily newspapers reach a large proportion of middle and lower income groups but are read by only a few of the wealthy.

Weekly papers are read primarily by residents of small towns and rural areas. Income and educational levels are often low.

Newspapers have a very short lifetime, usually less than a day. "Nothing is older than yesterday's newspaper" is a conclusion shared by practically everyone. Friday, Saturday, and Sunday editions are more carefully read and are the best days for you to advertise if your product or service has a broad appeal. Sunday is the best of the three days. Evening papers are better than morning papers from the advertiser's viewpoint.

The typical newspaper is read by a number of persons having a wide range of interests. If your product or service appeals primarily to sportsmen or auto buffs, for instance, you will not usually reach enough of them to make newspaper advertising worth its dollar cost. (This cost is calculated on the basis of how much each *reply* to your ad costs.) Conversely, if your product or service is likely to be wanted by the average person, then the newspaper can be a profitable medium to use.

There are certain advantages in newspaper advertising which cannot be offered by magazines. The newspaper is usually less expensive, depending on its circulation. It is quick; you can place your ad one day and it will appear the same day or the next. You can reach a large number of people in a limited area in a hurry. You can change your ad as often as you wish, to test the pulling power of your words. And you can test differently worded ads by using several newspapers at the same time.

USING NEWSPAPERS TO TEST YOUR ADS

The advantages which newspapers have can greatly aid you in starting your mail order business. You can test differently worded classified ads placed under several classifications rapidly and inexpensively before you begin to advertise in magazines.

It is impossible to forecast the numbers of replies you will receive. However, you can anticipate that from 3 to 10 persons per 1,000 circulation will be interested in what you have to offer. This means a probable minimum of 300 replies from a newspaper with a circulation of 100,000; 3,000 from a circulation of 1 million, etc.

Not all persons who reply to your ad will actually buy, of course. Much depends not only on your product or service but also on the effectiveness of the follow-up advertising material you mail to each correspondent. A reasonable estimate of buyers might be from 1 to 10 percent, but usually below 5 percent of the number of replies to your classified ad.

During the period in which you are using newspapers to test your ads, you will be more concerned with discovering which ad pulls the most replies, rather than the actual number of orders you receive. If one ad consistently brings in more replies than the others, *based on circulation in similar markets,* it can be assumed that this ad is the best of those you are running. It then becomes the prime candidate for your magazine advertising campaign.

An ad placed in a Chicago paper can be compared with one placed in any other large city daily paper, but not with one placed in a small town paper. For comparisons to be valid in ad testing, the markets must be as similar in as many ways as possible.

MILLINE RATE

There is a way to compare one newspaper against another for effectiveness before you advertise, although this method necessarily ignores the quality of the markets. But it does enable you to compare a small town newspaper with one in a metropolitan area and it is valuable for this reason. This method compares the *milline rate* of each newspaper. The milline rate is readily determined by taking the line rate (the price the newspaper charges per line of your classified ad), multiplying it by 1,000,000 and then dividing by the circulation of the newspaper. The computation is really quite simple:

$$\text{Milline rate} = \frac{\text{Line rate} \times 1,000,000}{\text{Circulation}}$$

To get the line rate, simply write the director of advertising at the newspaper, who will be more than happy to send you a rate card. To compare Newspaper A having a line rate of $1.20 and a circulation of 923,247 with Newspaper B having a line rate of $0.75 and a circulation of 375,240, we find, using the above formula, that Newspaper A has a milline rate of about $1.28 and Newspaper B has a milline rate of about $1.98. It is obvious that Newspaper A, *although it has the highest line rate, has the lowest milline rate and thus it is the least expensive of the two newspapers.* In other words, despite the higher cost of your ad, it will reach more readers at a *lower cost per reader* than would a cheaper ad in Newspaper B. Of course, this milline comparison disregards the type of audience each newspaper reaches.

When comparing two newspapers with the milline formula, that paper having the *lower milline rate* will be the less expensive on a per reader cost basis. If the quality of the markets is similar, as it would be with the *St. Louis Post Dispatch* and the *Kansas City Star,* choose the newspaper with the lowest milline rate.

The dollar figure expressed by the milline rate is an artificial figure used solely for comparison purposes. The milline formula enables ready determination of comparable costs of reaching readers. The formula is easy to use since you do not have to work with minute fractions of one cent, as you would if you determined the actual cost of reaching one reader by dividing the line rate by the circulation. A mistake in placing the decimal point could, in this latter instance, result in an error, another reason the milline rate is usually used to compare publications.

Some newspapers charge by the word, not by the line. In this case you would simply calculate a milword rate. But be sure not to compare the mil*word* rate of one newspaper to the mil*line* rate of another.

THE COST OF A NEWSPAPER CLASSIFIED AD

Space in newspaper classified sections is normally sold by the *agate line*, so the cost of your ad will depend on how many lines long it is. There are 14 agate lines to the inch. A dime will cover approximately 10 agate lines. One agate line contains approximately five average length words. Since classified ads are charged for by the line, if the line rate is $1.80, the approximate cost of the final 24-word classified ad illustrated in chapter 5 can be found as follows:

Headline (4 words) requires 2 agate lines	3.60
Body copy (20 words) uses 4 agate lines	7.20
Name, address (8 words) uses 2 agate lines	3.60
Total	$14.40

The sample ad is repeated below as it would appear in the newspaper. The phrase *Desk R* is a key which identifies the publication. Keys are explained later in this chapter.

NAME YOUR OWN INCOME

NO SELLING. Work home. Guaranteed. Profits daily. Grow big fast. New book reveals secrets, tells how. Free details. Write now. Burnside, Desk R, Box 910, Dover, DE 19901.

The headline is centered and printed in heavy, boldface capital letters larger than the rest of the ad. Most newspapers automatically set the first word or two of body copy in capital letters at no additional charge, as shown above. The entire ad requires less height than can be covered by a dime. Larger sizes cost more but may not pay. *A small ad with impact will usually make a profit.*

ESTIMATING AD LENGTH WITH YOUR TYPEWRITER

The cost of your classified ad will depend upon how many lines long it is. Of course, if you want special-looking type or special spacing, this will add considerably to your cost. But we are assuming a simple classified ad of one headline and several ordinary lines of type.

To figure out how many lines of type your ad will take up in the newspaper, you want to be able to type your ad so the typewritten ad has the same number of characters (letters and spaces) per line as it will in the newspaper. In order to do this, you will have to do a little measuring and counting.

Many newspapers have a classified column width of 1⁹/₁₆ inches, while others will have a column width that is slightly wider or narrower than this. Whatever the width of the classifieds column in the newspaper in which you wish to advertise, it is relatively easy to figure out how long you should type each line of your ad so it will have the same number of characters per line as it will in the newspaper. All you need to know is the average number of characters per line in the newspaper. Simply count all the letters, punctuation marks, and spaces in three lines of a sample ad in the paper, and divide that number by three. Now you have an *average* number of characters per line in that newspaper column. (You can probably see that it is best not to count characters in three lines that all look very crowded, nor in three lines that all look very open. After all, you are aiming for an average.)

Now you can set up your typewriter so it will type that same number of characters per line. Put a piece of paper in your typewriter and type the letter X as many times as the average number of characters you obtained. Remove the paper and draw two lines down the length of the paper. Your row of Xs shows how far apart to draw the lines. Now you have your own "newspaper column" and can type in your ad.

Having set up your dummy oversize column on blank paper, put the paper in your typewriter so the left margin is at the left-hand border of the column. Now type your ad, doing your best to use the entire column width without too much over-run or too many short lines. Over-runs and short lines tend to average out over an ad several lines deep, so don't be too concerned over minor discrepancies. Be sure to include your company name, address, and zip code since these must appear in the printed ad.

Count the number of lines in your ad. Be sure to add one additional line to provide space for your headline. Now look at your ad closely. Are over-runs balanced with short lines? Is your last line a half column width or less? If the answers to these two questions are "Yes," your printed ad will occupy the number of lines you calculated. This total is the number of lines you should pay for when mailing your check with your ad. If there are more over-runs than short lines, and especially if your last line is almost a full column width, your ad will probably run over into an extra line. Your cost will increase slightly.

MAGAZINE ADVERTISING

Because most magazines are directed to readers with particular or special interests or characteristics, ads placed in the right magazines can represent your best advertising dollar buy. There are three distinct main groupings of magazines in the United States: general interest magazines, class magazines, and trade and professional magazines.

General interest magazines include such publications as *Reader's*

Digest, Saturday Evening Post, Newsweek, etc. They appeal to a very broad cross-section of the public. Usually included in this group are the major women's magazines such as *Good Housekeeping* and *Redbook.* Few if any of these magazines accept classified ads, and their prices for illustrated display advertising are far higher than any but a successful and well-established business could afford. However, they are excellent places to advertise a product or service which has great appeal to most persons. The smallest ad usually accepted is *one column inch,* a space the full width of a single column and one inch in height. Rates are quoted per column-inch instead of by the line as in classified ad pages.

Class magazines include the majority of those published every year. They appeal to distinct segments of the public. Some magazines typical of this group are *Popular Mechanics, Popular Science, Car and Driver, Parents, Organic Gardening and Farming, Yachting,* and *Sports Illustrated,* but there are many, many others. No matter what your product or service or the market you wish to reach, there will be at least one and probably several magazines within this group tailor-made for your ad campaign. These are the magazines you will probably want to use.

Trade and professional magazines are published for people in practically every line of work from advertising to zoology. They are usually circulated on a subscription basis and rarely appear on newsstands. If your product or service is of primary interest to engineers, ironworkers, bakers, store managers, or other similar groups, you should consider advertising in appropriate trade publications. Your public library subscribes to many of these publications and also has directories which list several thousand different magazines.

The magazine ad often exhibits a remarkable life, bringing replies months and even years after the month in which it was published. Magazines are often kept around the house.for months. Too, magazines are read or glanced at by many more persons than those who initially buy them. In most cases you can anticipate receiving the bulk of replies from an ad in the month following the date of publication, with reduced numbers during the following two months or possibly three. Occasionally you will receive replies based on ads that ran six months, a year, or even more in the past. In many instances these inquiries resulted from readership of older magazines in the waiting rooms of doctors, dentists, and other professional offices.

CHOOSING EFFECTIVE MAGAZINES

As you select magazines for advertising, you will want to compare the type and size of their readership and their advertising costs. The circulation figures of most magazines are available to you as an advertiser. These figures are accurate since most are subject to audit by the Audit

Bureau of Circulation. They show, among other things, the number of subscription copies mailed and the number of copies sold on newsstands. These two figures are the only ones of interest to you.

Note particularly the number of newsstand copies sold. People buy magazines at newsstands because *they want the magazine.* The larger the number of newsstand copies sold the greater the *interested readership* your ad will have.

The number of newsstand copies sold is often of greater interest than the number of subscriptions for several reasons. Subscriptions to many magazines can be obtained at very reduced prices from subscription agents all over the country. Many subscriptions are received from friends and relatives as gifts. When a magazine can be subscribed to at much less than the usual subscription price, the reader tends to downgrade its value and doesn't pay as much attention to its contents as he would if he paid the normal price. Gift subscriptions, too, often represent more closely the taste of the giver than the interests of the recipient and thus have less apparent value to the reader. Furthermore, many families subscribe to a number of magazines. These magazines often pile up almost unread, sometimes because of lack of real interest and often because there are more magazines than time to read them.

For the reasons given, the figures representing subscription copies may not fairly represent the real magazine readership. They should be somewhat discounted. On the other hand, when you buy a magazine on the newsstand you buy it because you are interested in something in it and intend to read it soon after purchase.

Newsstand circulation figures mirror actual, interested readership very accurately. Look for magazines with high newsstand sales for your most effective advertising, regardless of subscription figures.

Your library has in its reference section Standard Rate and Data books which give advertising rates and column widths for every magazine and newspaper in the country. Rate books are published for radio and television stations as well. Checking these sources will guide you in estimating the cost of your ads in these various publications. Comparing similar publications using the milline rate formula discussed earlier will help to guide your advertising expenditures to those publications which produce the best coverage per dollar spent for your ads.

Another valuable source of information is the *Directory of Magazines with Classified Ads,* available from SpeciaList, 134 Manchester Road, Ballwin, MO 63011. It lists names, addresses, and word and/or line rates, plus circulation figures, for what seems to be all the magazines published in the United States which accept classified and small display ads. Current cost is about $10. If your area stores or local library are not well stocked with special-interest magazines, this directory can introduce you to them. Many magazines will provide free sample copies where they are not available locally, and all will respond to queries regarding advertising rates.

The milline rate formula for comparing newspaper advertising costs can readily be used to compare magazines; thus you will be assured of the most exposure for the least dollar cost. However, your cost comparison will be meaningful only if you compare magazines having similar audiences. This is easy to do since a number of magazines compete in the same fields.

You can safely compare the milline rates of *Yachting, Sea, Motorboating & Sailing,* and *Boating* if what you offer appeals to small boat owners. You can compare *Field and Stream, Outdoor Life,* and *Sports Afield. Popular Mechanics, Mechanix Illustrated,* and *Science and Mechanics* also appeal to similar markets.

In almost every special interest group imaginable there are several magazines competing for readers. This tends to keep advertising costs competitive. Because these magazines do compete for readers, you may wish to insert ads in more than just the one magazine having the lowest milline rate.

You should be aware, however, that there is some overlap in readership between similar magazines, with some persons reading two or more magazines in the same field. This means that your ad in two or more related magazines will be seen by some of the same readers. Results of multiple magazine insertions are difficult to evaluate. The mere fact that people see your ad in more than one magazine will cause some persons to reply who might not have done so when they first saw your ad. Or they might have missed your ad in one magazine but noticed it in another.

Overlap in readership also means, of course, that your ads are not reaching the number of *different* readers as the sum of circulation figures would indicate. But since you will always reach some readers through one magazine who are missed by another, you will get more replies by advertising simultaneously in several related publications. Whether this is financially worthwhile depends on your cost per reply. This aspect of your business is considered later in this chapter.

To help select the right magazine or magazines for your ad, either purchase copies of several magazines which you feel are probably read by the type customer you wish to reach (the cost of purchase is a tax-deductible business expense) or read them at your public library. Be sure the magazines you investigate carry classified ads before you buy them or spend time going through them. You will initially be advertising only in magazines which carry a good selection of classified ads.

First look over the classifications in the ad pages of each magazine. If others offer something similar to your product or service, this means that some of the readers buy these items. At the top (usually) of the first page of classified ads, the rate will be given, per word or per line. Also given are options and prices for special treatment including headline, heavy type, block letters, and possibly others. Note these on a card for future reference. (This same information is contained in Standard Rate and Data books discussed earlier.)

Also note the deadlines specified for classified ads, usually from one to three months prior to publication. If the magazine has a three-month deadline, your ad must reach the magazine in September to appear in the January issue. A one-month deadline means your ad, sent to the magazine in November, can appear in the January issue. In both cases the January issues are actually printed and distributed in December.

Read all the ads in all the classifications applying to your product or service. This gives you a feel for the number of possible competitors you may have as well as their ability to write an interesting ad with strong emotional impact.

Read the stories and articles. Each of these is published because the editor believes they will interest the readers. These stories give you clues to the type person who will be attracted to the magazine and also to his educational and economic background. Characters in stories and person-alities in certain articles are *sometimes* similar to the average reader. More often they represent the reader's dreams, the type person he would like to be or the situations of which he would like to be a part. Remember the average man's Walter Mitty complex. A review of chapter 1 as you read these magazines will aid you in picturing the needs, desires, and personality of the average reader of each particular magazine.

TIMING YOUR ADS FOR MAXIMUM RESULTS

Statistics show that more ads are read during January, February, September, October and November than in other months. This is partly caused by the weather and normal vacation schedules in the United States. The best advertising months are those of fall and winter when chill winds begin to blow, the days are shorter, and people become interested in acquiring things in preparation for winter. They are generally more receptive to all kinds of advertising and less hesitant to buy something which interests them. When spring and summer arrive, people instinc-tively forget another winter is not far away. They play and enjoy the fine weather and warm sunshine. Rarely do they look beyond the present. For these reasons these months are not the best for advertising. Because the reader is able to seek enjoyment and recreation outside the home, he spends much less time reading and pays less attention to what he sees. His thoughts are elsewhere. Proof of this is in the rather poor and repetitive programming on television during these months. Television advertising is among the highest priced media, and smart advertisers do not waste money trying to reach an audience which isn't there.

The month of December is not a good month to advertise mail order items despite its being a winter month. To most people December means Christmas or Hanukkah and little else. From Thanksgiving until after New Year's, the average person is not a reader of classified ads. His purchases are practically all made over the counter at local stores. He cannot wait for a mail order to be processed. He is too busy to bother with placing an order with you. His dislike of writing letters, coupled with the necessity of sending out greeting cards, means you stand little chance of convincing him to mail you an order or even an inquiry.

The bulk of your advertising efforts should be confined to the good months of January, February, September, October, and November. Your message should be placed in the hands of potential customers during these months.

Most magazines are distributed one or more months *earlier* than their cover dates. You must know this distribution schedule and the deadline for ads for each magazine. This information is essential to proper planning and scheduling your campaign. If a magazine is distributed during the month preceding the cover date, as most are, and you want your ad to reach the public in January, you will have the following facts to consider:

The February issue of *XYZ Magazine* is published January 10, mailed to subscribers and distributed to newsstands a day or two later. The three-month deadline means your ad must be delivered to the magazine *before October 10*. You prepare your ad, including instructions that it shall be printed in the magazine's February issue under the classification you specify. Mail the ad with your check so that it reaches the magazine several days before the October 10 deadline. This means that in September you will be preparing an ad to appear in next February's magazine which the public will receive in January.

If you strictly follow the January—February—September—October—November formula, you will tend to get most of your orders and inquiries in February through March and October through December, with very few during the months of April to September. You should not let these months go to waste even though they are not the most productive. They can still produce more than enough business for you to bring in an additional profit, and they will partly smooth out your annual work load.

The best and most effective way of advertising throughout the year is specified below. It is assumed that your ads will appear in several magazines to reach the best and largest markets.

All magazines: January, February, September, October, November.
Half the magazines: March, May, July.
Half the magazines: April, June, August.

This method of advertising cuts costs during the less productive months, yet keeps your message before the public. A somewhat different yet effective method, which costs even less for advertising, follows:

Half the magazines: January, March, May, July, September, November.

Half the magazines: February, April, June, August, October, December.

This latter method of distributing your advertising is best applied to similar magazines in one or more specific fields such as outdoor sports, automobiles, boating, etc. It is somewhat less effective when applied to magazines of more general interest.

EXPERIMENTING TO FIND THE BEST AD

When you have developed the best ad you can, as described in chapter 5, you may or may not have the ad which produces the most replies, generates the most orders and produces the highest profits. If you feel the replies you get are at least average and about what you can expect, your ad is obviously a good one and any changes you make should not be drastic.

The best way to experiment is by dividing the magazines in which you advertise into two groups. Make a *minor* change in the ad and try it for one month in one of these groups. Try a different month for the other group, using the changed ad. A sudden rise or fall in replies resulting from this change will indicate whether your change is better or has an adverse effect.

The first and most logical place to experiment is in the headline which first catches the reader's attention. *Make only one change at a time* so that you will be able to determine what works and what doesn't. There should be only one small thing different from normal in your ad at any one time. Below are suggested experimental changes in the headline of the sample ad devised in chapter 5.

Normal, boldface	**NAME YOUR OWN INCOME**
Boldface, italics	***NAME YOUR OWN INCOME***
Boldface, quotes	**"NAME YOUR OWN INCOME"**
Boldface, dashes	**—NAME YOUR OWN INCOME—**
Boldface, exclamation	**NAME YOUR OWN INCOME!**
Boldface, word change	**YOU NAME YOUR INCOME**
Boldface, bullets	**• NAME YOUR OWN INCOME •**

The above suggestions are just a sampling of a few minor headline changes. Often such a small change can double the number of replies to your ad! There is no scientific way of determining what will work in any specific instance nor even of discovering why some inconsequential change can make such a large difference in an ad's effectiveness. Experimenting may give you the right answers.

When you have ceased experimenting with your headline, and your ad is drawing the maximum number of replies, you can *cautiously* experiment with the body copy. Again, it is most important to keep changes minor and to test changes against your normal ad in half the magazines you use. It is unnecessary to experiment further in your ad than those first ten important words of body copy.

Initial changes should consist of a rearrangement in the order of the points stressed. Considering only the first two lines of the sample ad developed in chapter 5, the following are a few of the possible changes which can affect the drawing power of your ad:

Normal   NO SELLING. Work home. Guaranteed. Profits daily. Grow big

Change #1   WORK HOME. No selling. Guaranteed. Profits daily. Grow big

Change #2   GUARANTEED. Profits daily. No selling. Work home. Grow big

Change #3   PROFITS DAILY. Guaranteed. No selling. Work home. Grow big

Note that in each case you can single out a specific point with which to start the body copy. This point will be reinforced by being set in all capital letters as is normally done in most classified ads. It will be preferable to keep mention of the daily profits and the guarantee adjacent so the reader will infer that the two go together, as explained in chapter 5.

Whatever changes you make, keep in mind that your ad must answer the reader's question, "What's in it for me?" By answering this question in as many ways as possible you hold his interest and reinforce his determination to act—by replying to your ad.

Eventually, if you are both skillful and lucky, your ad will have evolved to the place where it consistently brings in more than the average number of replies. Should you change it? No! A good ad today *which appeals to basic human nature* will still be a good ad years from today. As long as it works for you, even though you may not fully understand why, keep it running and keep the profits rolling in.

This does not mean you will never have to compose a different ad. You should always have some ads or ideas for new ones in reserve so you will not be left empty-handed should your current ad suddenly turn sour. This can and does happen through no foreseeable circumstances. It can be caused by world or national news events, new inventions, competitive advertising, and other, even more unusual or unknown reasons. While this is unlikely if your ad has strong basic appeal, it will still pay you to continue to experiment on a small scale. After all, your ad is good, results are better than average, and you have improved it as much as possible. But—how do you know how closely it approaches perfection? Is it possible to compose an entirely new ad which may work even better? Often it is, and this is why continuing experiments should be conducted on a small scale.

You can confine your experiments in composing an entirely new ad to one or two magazines while continuing to run your normal ad in the rest of the magazines as a control. *Normal and experimental new ads must both run in the same magazine at the same time and under the same classification.* Judge the returns from the experimental ad against your normal ad. If your revised ad brings in consistently more replies than the normal ad, run the new ad in another magazine or two. If it continues to draw well, and better than your normal ad, try to make it as good as you did with your first ad. When the new ad is substantially better in drawing power, you should gradually replace your normal ad with the new, improved ad in all the magazines you use.

Be sure to test your new ad against your normal ad *in each magazine* before making the change. The old ad might still be the best in some magazines. No one can tell you why, but if it happens, accept it. Whatever brings in the most replies makes the most sales and produces the greatest profits.

KEYING YOUR ADS

If you advertise in more than one periodical, or run two experimental ads in the same periodical, you will need to know which magazine or ad was responsible for bringing in each reply. Knowing the source of each reply will help you determine the effectiveness of your ads and the cost of each reply and each sale in terms of advertising dollars. Knowing these costs will help you direct your advertising campaign wisely and profitably.

To identify the source of each reply, you will want to key your ads. An ad key is a simple code placed in your ad. The code is different in each periodical in which your ad appears. The code also must be in a form your customer will be forced to include in his reply to you.

Many people are aware of codes in ads although they may not know the reason they are used. Unfortunately, some persons take a perverse pleasure in omitting the code when they reply if this is easy to do and your code is obvious. When you receive an uncoded reply, you are unable to credit its source and this makes it difficult for you to check accurately the cost per reply from each ad. Uncoded replies are usually distributed proportionally among the periodicals you advertise in at the end of each month.

There are numerous ways to code an ad if the ad itself or a coupon is not to be returned. Most of these codes are made a part of the address in one manner or another. Often an expression such as *Dept. 512, Floor L, Room 17,* or *Desk R* is included as part of the company address. Number or letter keys in your ads are different in each magazine or newspaper, of course. This method is not as effective as some others to be described, and also can be more costly if your ad is on a charge-per-word basis. It can also cause your ad to run over an extra line, thus costing you an additional amount for each insertion.

If you use your own name as a company name, use different initials to key ads in different magazines: *J. Smith, M. Smith, R. Smith.* This is excellent and your key is undetectable by the reader. It also does not increase the cost of your ad. Another way to key your ad is by adding a letter to the street number or post office box number: *Box 1833-R, 212-B Front St.* Be sure to check with your local postmaster for permission before using this method of keying. Usually you will get permission to do this, and this method provides from 19 to 23 different key letters from the alphabet. You should never use the letters *I, O,* or *Q* as a key since they are easily confused with numerals. Also, if you key your street number, never use the letters *E, N, S,* or *W* since they can be confused with directions.

Another method of keying which is rarely detected by the average reader is to key the material they will be asking for. Tell them in your ad to ask for *Booklet M, Brochure 2F,* etc. This method does increase the size and cost of your ads, however. The keying of requested material is also an excellent way to test the response from different mailing lists which may be rented or purchased for a direct mail advertising effort. Mailing lists are discussed in chapter 12.

Ads which contain a coupon which the reader is expected to return are usually coded with a letter and number combination placed in an open area of the coupon. Thus, a letter can be assigned to identify a specific magazine and a number (from 1 to 12) designating the month's issue in which the ad appears.

Most people, however, can't find cellophane tape to stick a coupon on the back of a postcard and will hesitate to hunt up an envelope and stamp. Coupons are used mostly so the advertiser can identify the publication in which the ad was printed. But as we have seen, keying can be done by other means much less expensively while still making it easy for your customer to reply.

YOUR COST PER REPLY AND PER SALE

The replies you receive to your ads cost you money—the money spent for classified ads—and while all replies are valuable, some may cost you more than they are worth. Keying your ads and knowing which periodical generates which replies makes it simple to determine what each reply costs you. This can be done easily, using the following simple formula:

$$\text{Cost per reply} = \frac{\text{Cost of ad in dollars}}{\text{Number of replies}}$$

As an example, your ad in *ABC Magazine* cost $24.30 and realized 261 replies in one month. Your ad in *XYZ Magazine* cost $18.25 and brought in 137 replies. Your cost per reply is:

$$ABC\ Magazine: \quad \frac{24.30}{261} = \$0.093\ (9\tfrac{1}{3}\ \text{cents})$$

$$XYZ\ Magazine: \quad \frac{18.25}{137} = \$0.133\ (13\tfrac{1}{3}\ \text{cents})$$

The cost per reply of approximately $0.093 from *ABC Magazine* is within reason. The $0.133 per reply which *XYZ Magazine* costs is high, and may be too high unless the persons replying to *XYZ Magazine's* ad consistently buy at least one-third more often than those answering ads in *ABC Magazine*.

Since the quality of replies (the percentage who eventually buy your product or service) varies between magazines, it is also important to determine what percentage of replies from each magazine results in sales. This is easily calculated. *Simply add two zeros to the number of sales, and divide by the number of replies.*

Assume 250 replies and 75 sales resulted from an ad costing $25:

$$\frac{7500}{250} = 30\ (\text{percent})$$

This 30 percent figure of sales versus replies is actually very high. A 5 percent figure would be closer to what most mail order businesses reasonably expect.

It is also of interest to determine the amount of your advertising dollar which each *sale* costs, since this affects your *profits* from each sale. To determine advertising costs per sale, the following formula may be used:

$$\text{Cost per sale} = \frac{\text{Cost of ad}}{\text{Number of sales}}$$

Using the same example as above, in which 75 sales (out of 250 replies) resulted from an ad which cost $25, the cost per sale is:

$$\frac{\$25}{75} = \$0.333 \ (33\tfrac{1}{3}\text{¢})$$

Of course, to know how many sales resulted from each ad, you must transfer the ad key to the order envelope you send to each inquirer. The ad key of each reply will be an important part of your record keeping, as discussed in chapter 10.

7

Your Follow-up Mailing

The classified advertisements you insert in periodicals have one basic result: they cause interested potential customers to write to you requesting additional information about your offer. These inquiries, the replies to your ads, are valuable in a number of ways. They contain the names and addresses of interested persons, and thus they represent the beginning of a two-way conversation between seller and potential buyer.

Your follow-up advertising, which is geared to making that potential customer *buy* your product or service, must be placed in the hands of your potential customer as soon as possible. This means it must be prepared, printed, and be ready for mailing *before* your first classified ad appears in print. You must be ready when replies come in and you should make every effort to mail your follow-up advertising materials within 24 hours after a reply arrives in your mail box.

The customer *was* interested when he replied to your ad. His card or letter took possibly several days to reach you, a delay you can do nothing about. But, don't add to this unavoidable delay. The customer's enthusiasm, as a result of reading your ad, tends to cool down with the passage of time. The sooner you can place your *real* sales effort in his hands, the better are your chances for making a sale. The sooner you reply to his request the more likely he will remember that he asked for it, thus lessening the possibility that it will be tossed out unread, as "just another piece of junk mail."

Your mailing pieces can take many forms (some of them are illustrated in figure 7-4). Cards, coupons, leaflets, folders, broadsides, envelopes, order blanks, pamphlets, brochures, samples, all can be used to present your message and get the order. You also have a choice of white or colored paper of different thicknesses and textures. You have a choice of typefaces, ink colors, and papers which your printer has available. You can decide design and layout of each mailing piece. In short, you have numerous sales advantages available. Not every style of mailing piece is needed for each specific product or service—you must select the choices best suited for you.

This chapter will discuss the purpose of your follow-up advertising (as you already know from writing your classified ads, the advertising must be geared to a specific purpose, or it will not succeed), and it will describe four basic mailing pieces that must be part of your follow-up advertising. Chapter 8 tells how to make use of advertising agencies and printers, and chapter 9 shows you how to do your own designing and preparation of low-cost, effective mailing pieces.

WHAT FOLLOW-UP ADVERTISING MUST DO

Regardless of the physical form it takes, your follow-up advertising is your real and most potent salesman. It goes into the homes where a welcome is assured since it was asked for. It thus has a great advantage over unsolicited advertising, commonly called "junk mail," which is often discarded unopened. It takes over where your classified ad left off. The customer wants more information: complete, detailed, and specific. You must give him this, always keeping in mind the customer's unspoken question: "What's in it for me?"

Your sales message is placed in the hands of a curious and tentatively interested potential customer. As he looks it over, it must first be physically attractive, well designed, and well printed. When he reads it you must maintain and intensify his interest, making him more curious while you satisfy his initial curiosity. Remember AIDA, the acronym for Attention—Interest—Determination and desire—Action, discussed in chapter 5? Your follow-up advertising must be designed to accomplish the same goals. It will be easier to do since your ad has already secured the customer's interest. Too, you have more space and can now use the psychological aspects of type, paper, color, design, and layout to reinforce your sales message.

Your follow-up advertising must hold and increase the customer's interest. It must answer his questions about your product or service. It must contain sufficient detail so he can decide if your offer is what he needs or wants. These details must excite his curiosity and make him want to know more, to own the product or use the service you offer, while they answer as many of his questions and objections as you can logically anticipate. It must prove in every way possible that your product or service is what your customer needs; that your offer is unique or better than anything else available; is inexpensive yet of highest quality; and can only be obtained from you.

Your follow-up advertising must also ask for the customer's order, making replying as easy and painless as possible. Four items must always be included in your follow-up advertising: (1) a postage-paid, self-addressed order envelope; (2) an order blank or order form; (3) a guarantee; and (4) your sales message. Each of these are discussed below.

THE ORDER ENVELOPE

You must make ordering as easy as possible, and therefore you should supply your potential customer with a printed, self-addressed order envelope. These can be prepared inexpensively for you by your printer. Envelopes may be either No. 6¼ Commercial (3½" x 6") or No. 6¾ Commercial (3⅝" x 6½"). Be sure they are opaque enough to adequately conceal the checks or cash that are contained in them.

Whether to paste a postage stamp on each return mail envelope or to use a business reply envelope depends both on the volume of your business and the ratio of orders to inquiries. At the time this is written first class postage is 15¢. Each inquiry you receive will result in your sending the customer 15¢ out of your pocket if you use postage stamps. Only some people will order from you. The remainder of the money you spend for return postage stamps is permanently lost.

On the other hand, a business reply envelope costs you nothing for postage until it is returned to you, at which time you pay the first class postage (15¢) plus an additional 5¢ per envelope, totaling 20¢ for each actual order. In addition, you must get a business reply mail permit from the U.S. Postal Service. Most printers can do business reply mail envelopes and will generally charge very little extra for this additional printing since it is all completed in a single operation.

Use of a business reply envelope will usually be the least costly in the long run. It also indicates to the prospective customer that yours is a recognized business and gives him the impression that you are large and well established. It has the disadvantage that it looks like any other business reply envelope and may thus be inadvertently discarded. It also lacks the urge to action presented by an actual postage stamp.

If a potential customer receives an envelope printed with your address and having a stamp properly affixed in the upper right hand corner, he is presented with a psychological dilemma. The average person is thrifty in small things and finds it extremely difficult to discard an unused stamp. The presence of the stamp tends subconsciously to impel him to use the stamped envelope. Thus he is pressed subconsciously to order from you, or at least to reply.

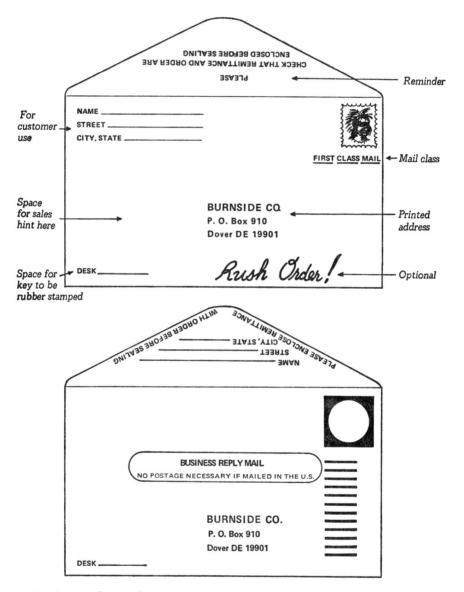

Fig. 7–1   Order envelopes.

He does not recognize this pressure and would deny its existence if it were to be suggested. Nevertheless, this real pressure exists. Whether it works in your favor depends on the effectiveness of your sales message, how badly the customer wants your product or service, and on its actual cost to him in dollars and cents.

Postage stamps will usually bring in more $5 orders than business reply envelopes and quite often are effective up to approximately $10, possibly more. *Reader's Digest* is one of the best-known users of postage stamps on return order cards and envelopes. The greater your margin of profit, the more you should consider postage stamps.

Typical order envelopes are illustrated in figure 7-1. Note the spot on the envelope for you to stamp the key of the ad to which your inquirer responded. When he sends in his order, you will then be able to match actual sales with particular ads. This will help you put your advertising dollars in the right place.

Not illustrated on the envelopes is the printing of optional sales hints which can be placed in blank areas of the envelope, front and back. A much different typeface should be used for these, and if the extra cost is justified, a contrasting ink color should be used. Red ink is excellent for phrases similar to those following:

Rush Order!
Here's my order. Process immediately.
Order enclosed. Please handle immediately.

In addition, on the back of each envelope should be printed *Thanks for your order* in large script-like type. Use either green ink or the same color ink used for printing the address on the face of the envelope.

THE ORDER BLANK

An order form must be enclosed either separately or as part of a larger piece of sales literature. If a part of your sales literature, it will not be easily lost, but a separate form is easier for your customer to use since he doesn't have to cut or tear it out of a larger piece of paper or card stock.

Here's a valuable hint. If you paste a label on the order blank already made out with the customer's name and address, you will receive more orders than if he has to fill it out himself, *because you made ordering easy for your customer*.

An order form is used if you are selling only one item, though separate order forms, one for each item offered, can be included if you sell a number of different products or services. Separate single order forms have two advantages. It makes it easy for your customer to order what he wants since he has only to fill in his name and address (unless you have

Burnside Co.
P. O. Box 910
Dover, DE 19901

☐ YES! Please rush my new book MAIL ORDER: STARTING UP, MAKING IT PAY by return mail. I am enclosing $0.00. You pay the postage. I understand you will refund my money if I am not satisfied for any reason and return the book to you within 10 days.

☐ Check here for free bonus for promptness

Miss
Mrs. ______________________________
Mr. Please Print

Street ______________________________

Apt. __________ Room ____ Rural Route ______

City ______________ State ______ Zip ______

ORDER FORM

Our Guarantee —

Read this valuable book without risk. If it does not meet with your complete satisfaction for any reason, return the book undamaged to us within 10 days and your money will be immediately refunded without question. The free set of business forms is yours to keep without obligation even if you decide you don't need the book.

Please rush my copy of your new book MAIL ORDER: STARTING UP; MAKING IT PAY by return mail. I am enclosing $0.00. You pay the postage. I must be satisfied or you will return my money in accordance with your guarantee.

Miss
Mrs. ______________________________
Mr. Please Print
Street ______________________________

Apt. ______ Room ______ Rural Route ______

City ______ State ______ Zip ______

☐ CHECK HERE FOR FREE SET OF BUSINESS FORMS IF YOU ORDER WITHIN 10 DAYS. Burnside Co., P.O. Box 910, Dover, DE 19901

Fig. 7–2 Order forms. Top: Coupon is part of the advertising material and is cut out by the customer. Bottom: Separate order form.

supplied a paste-down label) and possibly check a box or two. It also leaves blank order forms in your customer's hands for unordered items which he may purchase later.

A long order blank which the customer must fill in line by line with the item and its price is normally used only by companies whose products are so numerous that a small catalog is required to list them. Unless your business belongs in this category, eliminate such order blanks from your thinking. Use either a separate printed order form for each item or an order blank with *printed* prices and names of items and space for your customer to indicate how many of each he requires.

Typical order forms are illustrated in figure 7-2. An ordering price list is shown in figure 7-3. Note that there are a number of blank lines on the ordering price list. Additional items may be offered for sale without the

		BURNSIDE CO.	DO NOT WRITE IN THIS SPACE

Rush Order

BURNSIDE CO.
P.O. Box 910
Dover DE 19901

DO NOT WRITE IN THIS SPACE

ORDERED BY:

SHIP TO:

Miss
Mrs. _____
Mr.
Street _____
Apt _____ Room _____ Rural Rte. _____
City _____ State _____ Zip ____

Miss
Mrs. _____
Mr.
Street _____
Apt _____ Room _____ Rural Rte. _____
City _____ State _____ Zip __

QUANTITY	MERCHANDISE	EACH		TOTAL	
	BUSINESS FORMS , COMPLETE SET	O	OO		
	MAIL ORDER: Starting up, Making it pay	O	OO		
	TAX RECORDS FOR MAIL ORDER	O	OO		
	HOW TO WRITE SUCCESSFUL ADVERTISING	O	OO		
	Sales Tax				

Money Back Guarantee

All merchandise is guaranteed to be exactly as advertised.
Your money will be refunded if unsatisfactory merchandise is returned to us within 10 days.

TOTAL
ENCLOSED

**ALL MERCHANDISE
SHIPPED POSTPAID**

Be Sure to Enclose Your Remittance with Order

ORDER ON THIS FORM. Merchandise will be shipped to purchaser unless different shipping instructions are given in the space provided.

Fig. 7–3   Ordering price list.

necessity of having new order blanks printed. The block at the upper right is intended for the date the order is filled and the initials of the person preparing the order for shipment. Normally the order blank is enclosed with the merchandise as a packing slip.

YOUR GUARANTEE

Your guarantee is one of your most powerful selling aids. It should be prominent in your follow-up advertising and on your ordering form. Above all it must be truthful and you must stand solidly behind it. If you promise to refund money under certain circumstances, do so, even if you really can't feel too cheerful about it.

It is most important that you use simple, straightforward words in stating your guarantee. Use words your customer can understand completely the moment he reads them. Do not use flowery legal terms nor words which can have different meanings. Your customer must not only *understand* your guarantee; it must be impossible for him to *misunderstand* it.

Make the conditions under which you will make a refund very clear. It is also advisable to place a limit on the time allowed the customer to request a refund under the terms of your guarantee. This time limit should be reasonable, depending upon the price of the item and the value the customer will retain if he returns it. It also depends upon whether the item is fragile or easy to ship, etc. Usually seven to fifteen days will be a reasonable period to allow your customer to decide whether he wants to keep an item or return it for refund.

A guarantee which offers to refund the customer's money if he is not satisfied will always bring more sales than any other kind. Even though your guarantee is extremely liberal, you will rarely be asked for a refund. Unless your customer is thoroughly disgusted and feels he has been cheated, he will seldom make the effort required to wrap and mail the item back to you for refund. This was discussed in chapter 1. Also, unless your customer has invested a reasonable amount of money, he will probably toss the item out and absorb the loss rather than trouble himself with the bother of returning it. *Money-back guarantees will always bring in more profits.*

Several sample guarantees are described below. You may use whichever of these is applicable to your product or service and your method of doing business, or you may make up your own, using your own words. Make certain there is no chance of being misunderstood, however. Above all, keep it honest!

1. *If not satisfied, your money back within ten days.* This is as broad an offer as can legitimately be made. It means what it says. If the customer is dissatisfied *for any reason* his money will be refunded.

2. *Money refunded if* (merchandise) *is not exactly as advertised.* This is a tricky though perfectly legal guarantee. All it says is that your advertising accurately describes the merchandise. If the advertising is truthful, there is no way for the customer to get his money back. This is an example of how easy it is for the customer to read something into your words which they do not actually say. Be sure that *your* guarantee can be interpreted in only one way, that it does not suggest two or more different meanings.

3. *If not satisfied, return* (merchandise) *forthwith for refund.* This is another trickily worded guarantee. The hook is in the word *forthwith*, the legal meaning of which is "within 24 hours." This is usually too short a period to determine whether or not a customer is satisfied. It also is unfair

to expect the customer to understand obscure legal meanings of common words.

4. *You must be completely satisfied. If you find* (merchandise) *unsatisfactory for any reason, return* (it) *within 10 days and your money will be refunded without question*. This is a broad, simple, honest guarantee. The customer has ten days to decide whether he wishes to keep the merchandise. If for *any* reason he decides to return it within the ten-day period he may do so and his money will be refunded immediately. He does not have to justify his request for a refund but merely to ask for it.

5. *No risk 10-day trial. If for any reason you feel* (merchandise) *is not worth more than the price you paid, simply return* (it) *undamaged within ten days and your money will be refunded*. This is a broad guarantee which uses psychology to cause the customer to keep the merchandise and not ask for a refund. How can he determine accurately the dollar value of the merchandise, especially if it consists mainly of information or instructions?

6. *Try* (merchandise) *for 15 days. If you do not agree that* (it) *is the best available, return* (it) *for refund*. This is very trickily worded and guarantees absolutely nothing! It uses psychology to eliminate returns. The customer uses the item over a fifteen-day period and it is bound to become dirty, scratched, or otherwise damaged. He hesitates to return obviously damaged merchandise. Additionally, he is asked to agree that it is the "best available." What does *best* really mean? How can he know *everything* which is available? If he does decide to return it—and all the guarantee *says* is that he *can* return it—there is no assurance of refund. The guarantee does *not* say his money will be refunded but only that he can *return* the merchandise.

7. *Your money immediately refunded if* (merchandise) *unsatisfactory and is returned undamaged within 10 days*. This is an honest, straightforward guarantee. If the customer finds the item unsatisfactory for any reason and returns it undamaged within ten days his money will be refunded.

8. *If found unsatisfactory, return* (merchandise) *undamaged within 10 days and your money will immediately be refunded. You are the sole judge!* This is another honest guarantee which means exactly what it says. It further stresses that the customer makes the decision as to whether the merchandise is satisfactory. It shows the seller's great confidence in his product and has the psychological effect of discouraging returns. Who is he, a mere customer, to decide something is unsatisfactory when the seller so obviously feels it is excellent, a seller who knows much more about his product than the customer can possibly discover in ten days?

9. *Read this book for 7 days. If found unsatisfactory return it undamaged at the end of this period and your money will be refunded by*

return mail. This is a good, honest guarantee for book sales. It instills confidence in the book and in the seller, and definitely states the customer will not have to wait for a refund. Very few books will be returned if this guarantee is given.

Do not use the phrase *money cheerfully refunded* in your guarantee. No one refunds money cheerfully when it means a dissatisfied customer and a lost sale. The Federal Trade Commission is well aware of this and this phrase is being dropped because of the consumer interest in the Truth in Advertising Act.

YOUR SALES LETTER OR FOLDER

Your sales message is the most important portion of your follow-up advertising. It is carried by the mailing piece you select—and your choice need not be restricted to either a letter or folder. As illustrated in figure 7-4, the physical form of the mailing piece can vary considerably.

There are six main forms used by the majority of mail order advertisers. While not all may be applicable to your product or service, some will be. Two or three should be selected to use in your sales campaign, regardless of what your product or service might be. Following are the six basic forms of mailing pieces:

1. Sales letter
2. Insert
3. Single-fold folder
4. Multiple-fold folder
5. Die-cut novelty
6. Broadside

SALES LETTER

A sales letter presents your sales message in the form of a letter one or more pages long. The letter is printed on your letterhead or facsimile. The typeface used generally looks as if the letter is typewritten, although other typefaces are often used. The sales letter may be printed with black ink on white or colored stock (paper), or colored inks can be used.

The sales letter may occupy one or both sides of the paper. It can be included as part of a multiple-fold folder or broadside or may be in the form of a separate letter. The sales letter should not be more than two pages long, and a one-page letter can be even more effective than a longer one. Multiple-page letters are seldom read through. The average reader's interest is usually not sufficient to cope with the boring prospect of solid, unrelieved type.

You can present a large amount of information on a single typewritten

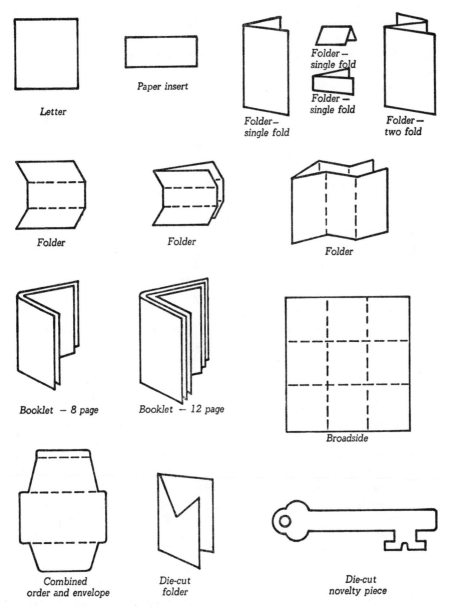

Letter

Paper insert

Folder— single fold

Folder— single fold

Folder— single fold

Folder— two fold

Folder

Folder

Folder

Booklet — 8 page

Booklet — 12 page

Broadside

Combined order and envelope

Die-cut folder

Die-cut novelty piece

Fig. 7–4 Some types of mailing pieces for follow-up advertising.

sheet, single spaced. Between 500 and 600 words can be typed on one side of standard 8½" x 11" paper with one-inch borders all around. Because of the space taken by the heading and signature, you will be able to get between 300 and 450 words in the body of your message. If you stop to consider how much you managed to convey in the 24-word classified ad described in chapter 5, you will realize how much more you can do with 300 or 400 carefully chosen words.

The sales letter is seldom used alone. Usually one or more different mail pieces are combined with the sales letter to more effectively present your message.

INSERTS

The paper insert is a single sheet of paper of a size to fit a No. 10 (business-letter size) envelope. It also may be slipped into a folder or broadside which can be mailed without an envelope.

You have a choice of paper thickness, quality, and texture; of the colors of paper and ink; of the design of the piece; and of the typefaces used.

The paper insert is an inexpensive and versatile form for a mailing piece. As many different inserts as necessary can be printed, and changes, eliminations, or additions are much less costly and result in much less waste than with any other form of mailing piece.

The insert is subordinate to other forms you may use. It lends itself well to order forms, warranties, guarantees, single-item advertising when you sell a number of products, special offers, etc.

SINGLE-FOLD FOLDER

A small single-fold folder of stiff paper or thin card can be your main mailing piece. The folder requires no envelope and can contain inserts, an order form, and envelope when closed with a seal, tape, or a staple. (Most people, however, dislike staples.)

Two basic shapes are available: tall and thin with a vertical fold, or more nearly square if folded horizontally. The vertical fold is recommended if the folder is to be mailed without an envelope. The horizontal fold is most applicable to a luxury item or a service business since it can be made to resemble a formal invitation to a party.

The total area available for your sales message on this type of folder is approximately three-quarters of both sides of a standard 8½" x 11" sheet of paper. If mailed without an envelope, space must be left for addressing and stamping, further reducing the space available for copy and artwork. However, there is more than enough space for most messages, especially when the folder is combined with inserts which emphasize sales points or point out the availability of different items.

MULTIPLE-FOLD FOLDER

Your imagination is the only limiting factor when you design a multiple-fold folder. Size and the number and direction of folds can be anything within reason, although a four- or six-page folder is used more often than larger, more complex designs. This is a highly effective method of presenting your sales message in an attractive manner. It is applicable to any type of product or service business.

A four-page folder opens out into a sheet 11" x 17", equal to two standard sheets of 8½" x 11" paper, and both sides can be used for your message. A six-page folder can give you even more space—but check with your printer for the most economical size of paper.

The first page of a multiple-fold folder can easily carry a sales letter on a facsimile of your letterhead. This can be a more personal, welcoming, and less imperative letter than if it were printed on a single sheet.

The inner two facing pages of a four-page folder give you a full 11" x 17" area in which to present the body of your sales message. Simple artwork and display type combined with copy blocks, with all words and phrases carefully chosen, make an extremely effective presentation.

The final page of a four-page folder (or the back two pages of a six-page folder) can sum up your selling points, contain an ordering coupon, and have space for postage and addressing.

Inserts, order forms, and reply envelope can be stuffed into such folders before mailing, making a mailing envelope unnecessary. (But using an envelope can be advantageous, as discussed later in this chapter.)

DIE-CUT NOVELTIES

A typical die-cut novelty is illustrated in figure 7-4. These can be produced in practically any shape, the printer using steel rule dies in his press. These dies cut the paper or card stock in the desired shape. Standard dies are available in such shapes as playing card spots, circles, ovals, crowns, anchors, boats, shoes, caps, hats, animals, and many others. Dies can easily be made in the shape of your product: spark plug, aerosol can, brush, radio, or other simple shape.

These novelty items are made of stiff paper or card stock and often are colored. Some are printed with a photograph of the product on one side and a sales message on the other. Others are printed with slogans and selling points. These can be cut of folded stock so they become small folders, or of a single thickness of card.

Novelty items can carry your advertising and be useful to the customer as well if they are printed as a ruler, for example, or contain temperature or metric conversion tables, decimal-fraction equivalents, drill sizes, or anything else which the customer will find useful. It should also tie in with your product or service or at least bear some relation to it. Some examples of novelty and product tie-ins are listed below:

Air pressure vs. tire sizes (auto accessories)
Temperature conversion scales (weather instruments)
Drawings of knots and splices (boating equipment)
Plug and point gap dimensions (auto accessories)
Height and weight tables (health or exercise products)
Currency converter (travel books or luggage)
Proofreader's marks (writing books, typing service)
Lumber tables (wood working tools and accessories)
Hunting and fishing data (sporting goods)
Drill sizes and equivalents (machine tools and accessories)

There are many more subjects for tie-in advertising than the few mentioned here. Something will be appropriate no matter what your product or service. Look for something simple and inexpensive to reproduce and useful to your customer which also ties in with your product or service. Select something novel or not readily available to the average person without his having to do some digging. You do the digging for him and your profits will go up with tie-in advertising novelties.

BROADSIDES

A broadside consists of a large sheet of paper, usually newsprint, printed on both sides and folded into a size suitable for mailing. A broadside is usually about the size of a single newspaper page. Often it is printed with headlines and columns to closely resemble a newspaper. Occasionally photographs or drawings are reproduced. Each column is broken up repeatedly by heads in large type as in the usual newspaper page.

A broadside lends itself extremely well to telling the story of your product or service in the main headline as well as in the columns of print, which are written as if they were actual newspaper news stories. The pictures or drawings and their captions will also help emphasize your sales message.

The broadside can carry several display ads for your product or service much as ordinary newspapers carry ads for department stores and auto dealers. This can be quite effective. An order blank can be printed on the broadside for the customer's use, although he will have to supply an envelope and stamp unless you include one. You can also print a business reply envelope and order blank combination. The customer can cut this out, fill it in, fold it, insert his remittance, and seal it with cellophane tape or a staple.

A broadside is also an excellent place to print excerpts from the testimonial letters you will begin to receive soon after you start your business (see chapter 11 for more on the use of testimonials).

THE MAILING ENVELOPE

Your follow-up mailing to each person who replies to your classified ad should consist of at least the following items: (1) the printed folder presenting your sales message; (2) the order envelope addressed to you, either business reply or stamped; (3) an order slip; (4) and a novelty item, if desired.

Sometimes you can skip the outer mailing envelope and just insert the order envelope, order form, and novelty item inside your printed folder, and seal or staple it shut. Your folder serves as your envelope. As a matter of interest, however, if you enclose your follow-up mailing pieces in an envelope, you can expect up to ten times as many orders as you would receive from mailing the folder with its enclosures as a self-mailer without a covering envelope. Many large direct-mail tests have been made to compare results between self-mailers and identical material enclosed in an envelope. In almost every case the use of an envelope resulted in more orders received. Increases were reported as high as ten times as many orders from sales appeals sent in envelopes.

Always enclose your follow-up mailing pieces in an envelope. It pays much more than it costs!

8

Advertising Agencies and Printers

WHAT AN AD AGENCY CAN DO FOR YOU

The advertising agency has gathered in one place a number of people with varying degrees of expertise in the many phases of merchandising through advertising. Agencies vary considerably as to number of employees but size is not indicative of proficiency, nor is a Madison Avenue address proof of competency. Whatever size and wherever located, the ad agency's primary function is to *increase the sales and profits of the client at the lowest cost to him.*

To perform this function adequately, the agency must have a number of different talents available. This does not always mean several people with multiple talents, although many creative people are multitalented. One exceptional man or woman, supported by a clerical staff, can represent all of the necessary talents and be, in effect, a one-man ad agency. The talents needed are:

Ability to write hard-hitting, selling copy
Ability to choose and use words with emotional impact
Artistic ability to design attractive layouts
Graphic arts skills
Knowledge of the printing art and what it can do
Familiarity with typefaces, cuts, borders, etc.
Knowledge of design, balance, and color psychology
Knowledge of photography as applied to reproduction
Thorough knowledge of all media which could be used for the client's
 benefit. Examples of such media include radio, TV, newspapers,
 magazines, point-of-sale, billboards, signs, transportation cards,
 handbills, sky writing, direct mail lists, samples, novelties,

package inserts, telephone soliciting, paperback book insert cards, package design, and many others.

Understanding of customer psychology and ability to see through the customer's eyes

Honesty and integrity in dealing with the client, the media, and the customer

An advertising agency can perform many services for you. It can advise you regarding the best newspapers and magazines for your particular product or service. It can tell you exactly what the cost will be for each ad in each medium since they have on file all current Standard Rate and Data books and rate cards. The agency can place your ads for you (more about this below). The agency can give you good advice as to the effectiveness of your copy and designs, usually free if during casual conversation. The agency will charge you for this service if you request a thorough analysis, however.

An ad agency will write your copy, do the necessary art work, choose type, prepare mechanicals (the originals from which your advertising and sales materials are reproduced), and coordinate your advertising campaign, all for a reasonable fee. They will also order your printing and can often provide faster and better service than you could get through your own efforts. An ad agency which feels you have a potential profit-maker (and they should know) may prepare a complete presentation for you without charge in the hope that you will become a client. Often a smaller agency will work with a small or beginning business if its potential for sales growth looks sufficiently good. They will hold costs down as much as possible, looking for future business success for their profits.

THE AGENCY COMMISSION

The main source of income for an ad agency is the standard 15 percent commission paid by the media—radio stations, newspapers, magazines—for all advertising placed with them through an agency. *You, the client, do not pay anything extra for ads you place through an agency* since all media pay the agency commission.

For example, assume you are placing ads in two magazines. According to their rate cards, the cost of each ad is $100. You place one ad directly, accompanied by your check for $100. The other ad you have the agency place for you. The agency bills you for the insertion cost of the ad, namely $100, which is exactly what the magazine would have charged you if you had placed the ad directly with them. However, the agency receives a check for $15 from the magazine as its commission for placing the ad. In one case the gross profit to the media is $100; in the other it is only $85. The cost to *you*, the advertiser, is $100 in both cases.

Can *you* somehow place your ads at agency prices or collect the agency commission yourself? After all, a 15 percent reduction in media advertising costs sounds good to nearly everyone. The answer is a resounding *NO!* The media offer commissions only to legitimate advertising agencies *which they recognize* because this is one of the ways the media have found to increase their income.

Advertising revenue pays the full cost plus profits of radio and television in this country, and is a major factor in the income of newspapers and magazines. No newspaper or magazine could exist without advertising because without advertising periodicals would cost so much that no one would buy them. The agency commission is thus a legitimate business expense for the media and allows the agency to provide numerous services to you, the advertiser, without charge. As an advertiser you will actually benefit from this practice and can save considerable time, as well as postage, in using an agency to place your ads.

SHOULD YOU USE AN AGENCY?

Maybe you can use an ad agency to advantage—and maybe not. After your business grows to the point where the advertising effort is taking more of your time than you are willing to give, an agency can take this extra work load off your shoulders. If you are just starting and can afford to pay fees for the preparation of your advertising materials, an agency can be an important factor. It can contribute to the rapid growth of your business and increase your profits. If you are starting with little capital, it will probably be best to forget about agencies and do the best job you can. This book makes it easy for you to prepare your own advertising (see Chapter 9), and your printer will be able to offer you much valuable information without charge.

If you decide to go to an agency, for a number of reasons it is wise to place your business with a local agency. Not only is it good community relations to place business with local concerns, but communication is cheaper and easier between advertiser and agency if both are in the same vicinity. This proximity saves time and is generally more satisfactory for you.

A small, local agency, if it has the needed skills and talents, can often give more time and do a more effective job for clients at lower total cost. Small accounts, such as yours is likely to be at the beginning, are very important to the small agency. Such accounts never get lost in the shuffle competing for attention with multimillion dollar billings of major advertisers. The small agency has access to the same markets and the same media as the largest, at exactly the same costs. Fees for extra work by small agencies will generally be less than large agencies with their enormous overhead. Of necessity, large agencies must look to large accounts to sustain their overhead.

So, should *you* use an agency? You probably will want to as your business grows. Whether you should do so at the start will depend entirely upon whether you actually *need* the services of an agency. If you cannot prepare ads and mailing pieces which are effective, you need the help an agency can provide. But if you can do an effective job by yourself, and you will be able to if you follow the methods explained in this book, you do not need an ad agency.

You might, though, place your ads through one agency and allow it to collect the small commissions. This will engender good will in the local business community for you and your company. You also will receive valuable free advice from the agency as to media and even the wording and format of ads you place through them. You save on postage and mailing costs in placing your ads locally. You are getting valuable services without cost.

AGENCY BILLING PRACTICES

If you have a good credit rating, your agency will bill you at the end of each month. This billing will include the insertion price of the ads they place for you and the charge for any work you ordered or expenses you authorized them to incur in your behalf. This is normal business practice and eliminates your having to invest your capital in advertising until 30 days later.

In a successful mail order business, the profits earned from sales will sooner or later pay the agency costs and other expenses and leave a sizeable profit for you. Thus, you need *invest no money* for advertising purposes since it will be paid for out of sales. The agency is, of course, using their own money instead of yours until you pay your bill, another excellent justification for the agency commission.

THE JOB PRINTER

The job printer is a local businessman who operates a printing business. He is usually willing to tackle any job from handbills and wedding invitations through pamphlets and even books. Usually he can do anything which can be handled on his presses and other paper-handling equipment. He frequently offers several different methods of printing and reproduction; he can print on tissue paper or thick cardboard; he can print small pieces or large sheets. He can use any color ink. He can print drawings and photographs. He can reduce or enlarge most copy or artwork. He can print loose sheets or supply them in tablet pads. He can collate, fold, staple, sew, bind, trim, die-cut, emboss, and engrave. He can supply stock in any weight, finish, color, and quality. In short, your printer is your supermarket for all your direct mail advertising materials.

Your printer is one of your best advisers as to choice of paper stock; color of paper and inks; size of your brochures, forms, and envelopes; and, if he provides typesetting services, he can also guide you in selection of size and style of typefaces. (If he does not have typesetting services on the premises, he can tell you where to get them.)

There are basically two types of printing methods: letterpress and offset. In letterpress, the ink is transferred directly from metal type to paper. In offset, the ink is transferred from a type master or *plate* to an intermediate material and then to paper.

LETTERPRESS PRINTING

Letterpress is the oldest method of printing and was used by Gutenberg in Germany when he printed his famous Bible sometime before A.D. 1456. Basically the process has not changed, although it has been considerably improved in the 500 years since the publication of the Gutenberg Bible.

To print by letterpress, the copy you provide is first composed in metal type by a typesetter. The body copy is commonly composed on a Linotype machine, which has a keyboard similar to a typewriter and produces an entire line of type cast at one time on a metal slug. Other kinds of equipment are used to set display type for headlines. Each letter and punctuation mark is raised above the surface of the slug and is upside down and backwards so when it is printed it reads correctly. The slugs are locked together in a form, which is then mounted on the letterpress. Ink is applied to the surface of the type alternately with the paper upon which the printed *impression* is made. Electrically operated presses can print several thousand impressions (copies) per hour.

Letterpress is most often used for printing business cards, invitations, envelopes, letterheads, blank forms, forms which are interleaved with carbon paper, die-cut novelty items, broadsides, handbills, display cards, shipping cartons, etc. Letterpress is also used to provide several clean, sharp *proof* copies which will be used in preparing *camera-ready copy* for offset platemaking. Usually three proofs are supplied unless you specify differently.

OFFSET PRINTING

Offset printing is the most widely used method of printing today. It is fast, efficient, and capable of high-quality reproduction in large quantities at reasonable cost. Offset is used to print forms, form letters, brochures, pamphlets, newspapers, books, magazines, folders, illustrations, almost anything you could name.

In offset printing, your original *camera-ready* copy is photographed to obtain a negative. Light is passed through the negative to expose a metal or paper plate, and the plate is developed rather like film to produce the type image on it. The negative is stored for future re-use.

Offset plates, whether metal or paper, differ from the metal type used in letterpress printing in that they are smooth surfaced and the type on the plate is right side up and reads from left to right, just like a printed page. Furthermore, the type on the plate is made so it repels water and accepts an oily ink. On the press, the plate transfers the ink to a rubber mat, and the mat *offsets* the ink onto the paper to be printed.

Metal plates, usually made of a thin sheet of flexible aluminum, are more costly than paper plates, but they have long lives and can make thousands of impressions. They are used for long or repeated print runs where the copy is unlikely to require change soon. Metal plates are usually cleaned after a run is completed and stored for re-use.

Paper plates are inexpensive and are often used for short print runs of a few hundred to several thousand copies. They wear out and new plates must be made for the next print run. Paper plates are generally more widely used when the copy is expected to be changed from time to time, or for dated material which will not be reprinted.

Also available is a kind of paper plate which you can type on yourself. These are useful for printing small quantities of second chance sales letters or other advertising which you want to appear as typewritten. These are discussed in chapter 11.

The camera-ready copy that is photographed for offset plate making will usually consist of typeset material pasted in position on a piece of art board. This board is called a *mechanical*. The mechanical can be made from a letterpress proof that has been cut apart and the copy blocks pasted in position. But frequently copy for offset printing is not set in metal but is set in "cold type," using one of several methods of photocomposition. Photocomposition is a very versatile technique of typesetting. Type set by photocomposition is produced as black type on white paper, which is used just like a letterpress proof in preparing mechanicals.

Your typesetter or printer may make mechanicals for you, but using the proofs and a razor blade, T-square, and rubber cement, you can produce all your own mechanicals. Getting your copy set in metal or by photocomposition and then making your own mechanicals (discussed in detail in chapter 9) is a good way to obtain a great deal of leeway in the design of your advertising material while keeping costs at an absolute minimum.

LETTERPRESS VS. OFFSET

Should you look for a letterpress or an offset printer? This depends somewhat on what is available in your area, on what you want to print, and on relative cost. The cost of metal typesetting and letterpress printing depends primarily on the time required to set and correct the type. Thus, three proof copies of a paragraph or two will cost only a few cents less than 100 or 500 copies. But the small amount of type required for a letterhead or envelope can be set in metal and proofed in minutes, so for certain types of printing, such as top-quality letterheads, business cards, etc., letterpress can be the least costly method. Letterpress also reproduces the sharpest images, assuming the metal type is clean.

If there is a great deal of copy to be set, however, and large sheets or a large number of copies are to be printed, offset is usually cheaper than letterpress in the long run. Offset is always the least expensive printing method for sales and form letters. And as mentioned before, getting your copy typeset and cutting apart the proofs to make your own mechanicals helps keep printing costs to a minimum.

FINDING A PRINTER

To locate a printer, look in the yellow pages of your area telephone directory. Call some up and tell them what you have in mind (letterhead and envelopes, single- or multiple-fold folders, brochures, business forms, whatever). Ask if they can handle the job, or who they would recommend for it.

You will want a printer who has a press that will print a minimum size of 11" x 17", the size of a four-page mailing folder. If he also has larger presses, this is fine, but be sure he can do 11" x 17" work. He should also be able to provide negatives of your camera copy. If he must send this work out, you may be able to have negatives made at lower prices than your printer charges if you take your mechanicals where he would send them. This can avoid the 10 to 15 percent handling charge the printer usually adds to the cost of work he sends out.

Don't forget to check with your local newspaper. Practically all newspaper printing rooms have typesetting equipment, and, if they set in hot metal, one or more proof presses. Many will set your copy and display heads and print proofs for you very inexpensively, since little time is needed. They fit these small printing jobs in between their normal newspaper work. Most newspapers have a fairly good selection of type for you to choose from.

Local printing houses and typographers may charge more than your local newspaper for the same work, but they may also offer artwork, design, and layout services.

Once you have located a good printer, stick with him. Give him all your printing work. As your business grows, so will his, and you will always be assured of good, fast work.

CHOOSING TYPEFACES

Your job printer (or typesetter) will usually have a large selection of styles of type for you to choose from, and he can assist you in selecting appropriate typefaces for your mailing pieces. Generally you will want a standard, easy-to-read typeface for the body copy, and a display type for your headlines that is in keeping with the kind of product you are selling and the audience you are trying to reach.

There are two large families of typefaces—gothic (or sans serif) and roman. Roman type has small tails or finishing strokes, called serifs, at the ends of the letters. This book is set in a roman face. Sans serif or gothic faces have no serifs on the letters. Each typeface will usually have, besides the regular letters, a bold and an *italic* alphabet.

Typefaces are identified by name (Times Roman bold, Times Roman regular, Helvetica regular, News Gothic condensed, etc.) and by size, which is given in *points*. Picas and points are the standard units of measure in the printing industry. There are six picas to an inch, and twelve points to every pica. Type sizes may be as small as 5 or 6 points, or as large as 72 points (one-inch headlines) or even larger. For reference, newspaper classifieds are frequently set in 5½-point type, this book is set in 10-point type, the subheads are 12- and 11-point type, and the chapter titles are set in 24-point type.

The amount of space between lines of type is also an important consideration. Lines of type without any extra space between them (like most classifieds) are said to be set *solid*. On most of your follow-up mailing materials, however, you will want a little extra space between the lines of type to help the readability. Printers and typesetters refer to this space as leading (pronounced *leding*), and one or two points of leading between lines is typical. Leading can also be expressed by such phrases as "six on eight" or "eight on nine." These mean, respectively, 6-point type with two points of leading, and 8-point type with one point of leading.

Typefaces and size are selected not only for appearance and readability, but also to help fit the written copy to the space allowed. The smaller the typesize and the less leading, of course, the more words you can get in a certain space. Adjusting type size and leading to make copy fill a space is discussed in the next chapter.

CHOOSING PAPER

You should depend upon your printer to assist you in the selection of paper, weight, and finish. He can show you samples of many different colors and thicknesses as well as slick to rough surfaces. Consider his suggestions, keeping in mind your product or service.

While a fairly smooth-surfaced paper or card stock will be suitable for most businesses, a rough surface may be best for sporting goods, for example, and a hard, slick, *calendered* surface for feminine or luxury items. However, novelty finishes often are higher in cost and may not be any more effective than something less expensive and more standard. Unless you have experience in applied psychology and in advertising or decorating, you will probably be better off closely following your printer's suggestions.

As a general rule, 16-lb. stock is sufficient for sales letters, order blanks, slips, leaflets, envelopes, etc. A normal bond paper (*sulphite*, made of wood pulp with no cotton or other fibers added) will be adequate. You can even use newsprint paper for small items which will be stuffed inside an envelope or other cover, and this is the cheapest paper stock of all.

A calendered (slick and smooth) surfaced paper of 20-lb. or 24-lb. stock is good for four-page, three-fold mailing pieces and for those which will be printed with photographs where it is important to show fine detail.

Heavier card stock, from 60- to 120-lb. is useful for novelty items which will be die-cut, and for folders designed as self-mailers. You are advised to use your printer's wide knowledge of paper weights and finishes to your advantage.

Below are listed the more readily available paper types and finishes.

> *Newsprint.* Used primarily in newspapers, as its name suggests. A coarse, rough-surfaced wood fiber paper. Very inexpensive.
>
> *Book stock.* Not confined to book printing. Available in numerous weights and finishes. Book stock may be the best choice for out-of-the-ordinary products or services. Types and finishes are discussed below.
>
> *Antique.* Soft, bulky, and rough.
>
> *Text.* Used mostly in fine printing. May have some rag fiber content.
>
> *Vellum.* Smooth and expensive. Usually off-white or cream colored.
>
> *Offset.* Smooth and uncoated. Suitable for most uses. Often stark white in color.
>
> *Gravure.* Similar to newsprint but smoother and very absorbent. Used mainly in rotogravure sections of Sunday newspapers.
>
> *English.* Has a clay content and is smooth but not glossy. Not bulky. Used by many magazines.
>
> *Super.* A polished paper.
>
> *Coated.* Smooth, slick, glossy calendered paper. Relatively expensive.
>
> *Bible.* Tissue thin.
>
> *Writing stock.* A smooth paper which may also be calendered. Available also as *bond*, which is crisp and permanent and

sometimes contains rag fibers. It is available in *ledger*, a thick, rich, very expensive paper with a high rag content and excellent folding characteristics.

Cover stock. A heavier paper than book but with similar qualities and varieties. Excellent for folders and self-mailers as well as novelty items.

Cardboards. These include the bristols and coated blanks, very heavy and thick.

WHAT YOU SHOULD KNOW ABOUT COLOR

In general you will always be safe if you stick to white paper and black ink for the majority of mail order products and services. This combination is attractive, readable, and familiar to all. Without a sound knowledge of color psychology and behavioral motivation you should approach the use of colored stock and ink with caution.

The readability (legibility) of the ten most legible color combinations are given below. Black on yellow is the most legible; white on red the least.

Legibility	Ink	Paper
1	Black	Yellow
2	Black*	White*
3	Yellow	Black
4	White*	Black*
5	Blue*	White*
6	White	Blue
7	Green	White
8	White	Green
9	Red	White
10	White	Red

Naturally, your copy must be legible and easy for your customer to read. Your choices of color combinations should be focused near the upper portion of the preceding table, especially those starred. However, there are other things you must know about color and its effect on people.

The combination of yellow and black is a very striking one, but difficult to use successfully; thus its use is limited to a very few special occasions. Red and white together mean danger to many people and so is not the best choice. Red on white also is often used on notices of overdue bills.

Red, orange, and yellow are warm colors, with red urging to action. Green and blue are cool colors denoting calm. Grey is neutral. Purple has a hint of royalty, of luxury. Red items appear closer to the observer, while blue and green items seem more distant.

Light-colored objects seem larger than those dark in color. Vertical stripes make something seem taller while horizontal stripes make it seem wider. An area of small checks appears larger than the same area of large checks.

By a very slight margin, the favorite color of most women is red, with blue a close second choice. With men blue is first, with red a close second. Next in rank with both men and women are purple, green, and orange, in that order. Young children prefer warm, rich red, orange, and yellow. As they grow older their color choices remain the same, but they show a preference for tones, shades, and pastels, not the saturated colors so enjoyed by the very young.

Warm colors are often more effective during the colder months and cool colors during the summer. Cool colors also can help to promote goods and services which offer the customer peace of mind, security, etc. Warm colors sell goods which the customer must use physically such as sporting equipment. Yellow and green promote vacation items. Blue and green are good for boating equipment. Grey denotes sympathy and sorrow to many people and thus should be used with care if at all.

Color should be rich if colored inks are used. But colored paper should be selected in the more subdued and pastel shades. Properly used, a colored ink or paper can perk up your advertising at little or no extra cost. Unfortunately, a thorough discussion of color psychology is outside the scope of this book. If you are interested in learning more about the subject, you can find books in your public library which will provide you with in-depth information.

9

Designing and Producing a Single-Fold Folder

By designing, writing the copy, and creating the mechanical for a single-fold folder, you will readily grasp the fundamentals of follow-up advertising and the principles of designing individual mailing pieces. You can apply these principles to any size or style of mailing piece used in your follow-up sales campaigns.

There are several steps involved in producing a printed mailing piece. These steps are listed below, and each will be described more fully in the paragraphs that follow.

1. Determine size, style, and purpose.
2. Make a layout showing copy blocks, display heads, and art.
3. Write copy and choose typefaces.
4. Have body copy and display heads set and proofs printed.
5. Draw or locate illustrations.
6. Make your mechanical.
7. Take mechanical to your printer for plate making and printing.
8. Choose ink and paper.
9. Determine the number of copies to be printed. Instruct the printer as required to collate, fold, pad, punch, drill, sew, staple, etc. Arrange, if possible, to keep the negative when printing is complete.
10. Collect printed material and the negative. Store the negative for re-use.
11. Make your mailing.

SIZE, STYLE, AND PURPOSE

The paper from which our sample single-fold folder is made measures 6½″ x 8½″, and when folded once aling the 8½″dimension it is 8½″ x 3¼″ in size. This will easily fit inside either a No. 9 Official (3⅞″ x 8⅞″) or No. 10 Official (4½″ x 9½″) envelope, or may be mailed as is. The design to be completed in this example is intended to be mailed without an envelope to save time, cost, and postage.

MAKING THE LAYOUT

The layout is a plan of every page in your mailing piece, showing position of headlines, copy blocks, and art, and indicating the size and style of type needed. To begin a layout for the sample folder, first, on a sheet of ordinary 8½″ x 11″ paper, mark off a distance of 6½″ along the long side and cut the paper straight across at that point. Discard the smaller strip and fold the larger piece evenly as shown in figure 9-1. It will be 8½″ x 3¼″ after folding once.

SIDE 1

Side 1 will contain space for address and postage. It also must catch attention and remind your customer that he asked for this information. With the open side of the folder towards you, draw a vertical line 4½″ from the right end of side 1 (see figure 9-2). On the right-hand portion of side 1, draw the name and address of your company in the upper left, using large type (18 point, for example) for the name and smaller type (10 or 12 point) for the address (see your printer for samples of type sizes).

The notation "THIRD CLASS MAIL" should be set in small type with the bottom of the letters 1⅜″ from the top of the folder, with ½″ between the end of the line of type and the right edge of side 1.

In the lower left of the right-hand section of side 1 is a standard instruction to the postmaster, directing him to inform you if the piece is undeliverable and to give you the addressee's forwarding address, if known. This will cost you 25¢ each time a customer has moved, but it will keep his name and address alive on your mailing list. This phrase is

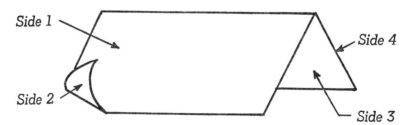

Fig. 9–1 Identifying the sides of a single-fold folder.

worded "ADDRESS CORRECTION REQUESTED" and is usually set in 10- or 12-point boldface sans serif type.

Normally an adhesive address label will be used to address the mailing piece, although it can be typed or written directly if you wish. Mailing labels are covered in chapter 11.

Now turn your attention to the left portion of side 1 in figure 9-2. The headline is in a large condensed script typeface. Its wording reminds the reader of your classified ad. The phrase, "It's easy," is a somewhat smaller typeface and is followed by three 8-point bullets (round black dots 8 points in diameter).

Below the headline is a block of copy. Actual body copy is not written out on a layout. Instead, the text is simply indicated by a box or a number of lines representing lines of type. This is customary when doing layouts.

The copy block on side 1 is used to quickly answer the reader's question, "What's in it for me?" This copy must be extremely visible and easy to read, so you will want to use a minimum of 8-point type and a maximum of 12-point type, and the lines of type should be leaded one or two points. Before writing the copy, the size of type and leading must be chosen and the proper number of words to fit the space must be determined. Copy writing and fitting copy to the available space is discussed in the next section.

Under the copy block is an arrowhead. In the white space to the left is a standard cut showing a handful of money. As discussed later in this chapter, there are numerous standard cuts or line illustrations available from which you can choose. You can also draw your own.

Sides 2 and 3

The inside of the folder, sides 2 and 3, is the showcase for your major sales effort. It is this 6½" x 8½" space which will gain another customer for you. Your primary job now is to effectively convince the reader that he *needs* and *wants* your product and that it offers him fulfillment of most of his unspoken desires at a very low price. In effect, *your* product or service is either unique (which is preferable) or is obviously the best obtainable on the market (which is quite satisfactory).

Sound impossible? Not really—not if you learn to do the right things and do them consistently. Look at figure 9-3, which shows an excellent treatment of the major sales effort. Now, how can you arrive at a similar result?

Open the paper folder you made and upon which you have sketched in the information and design of side 1. Treat sides 2 and 3 as a single space rather than two pages. With a folder this size, the area inside is too small to treat each side separately and still present your sales message properly. But when sides 2 and 3 are used as a single large space, you will have plenty of room to get your message across. You can use this space with the

Fig. 9-2 Layout for sample mailing folder—outside.

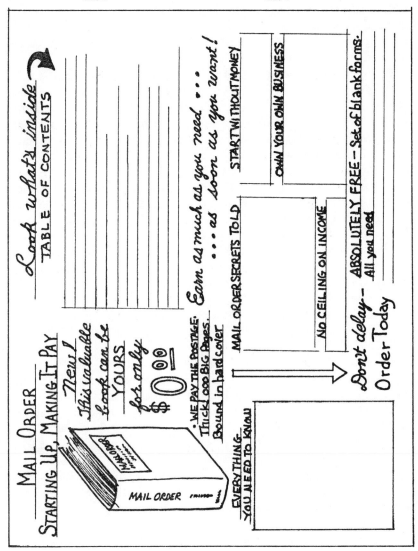

Fig. 9–3   Layout for sample mailing folder—inside.

long side either vertical or horizontal. In this example, because of the manner in which you will present your material, the space will be 6½" high and 8½" wide.

Lightly draw a vertical line dividing the space in half. The crease of the fold divides the space equally in the other direction. You now have four rectangles of equal size. You will *not* want to divide your copy so that the appearance is completely symmetrical. Symmetry denotes quiet, lack of movement. You want action!

While you do not want perfect symmetry, you do want balance. Solid areas of copy must be balanced by other areas of copy, but not necessarily of the same size. One large solid area can be balanced by a number of smaller areas. Solid blocks of type must be broken up by headlines, lines of display type. White space (areas not occupied by print or artwork) must be distributed so the visual appearance of the area is balanced. Figure 9-3 illustrates a well-balanced presentation.

In the upper left of side 2 is the title of the book in two lines, set in a large (24-point) condensed sans serif typeface. A sketch of the book appears beneath, and to its right other kinds of display type introduce the book in an attention-getting way. Below the price are three lines of smaller type describing the book and, briefly, the shipping conditions.

At the upper right the chapter titles are presented under the subhead "TABLE OF CONTENTS" which appears in bold capital letters. Above it is a large headline in a script face and a curved arrow.

At the lower left, under the drawing of the book, is a copy block 2" wide and 2½" deep under the boldface headline. "EVERYTHING YOU NEED TO KNOW." In this block you will place all of the most important points covered by the book. The space is quite restricted considering the amount of information which can be presented to prove to the reader that he needs and will receive great benefits from the book.

The headline in this example is very good. Any headline should be written to ensure that the block of copy beneath it will be read. With a well-written headline, you can afford to set the copy beneath it fairly small (even as small as 6-point type) to get the maximum number of words while still keeping the copy readable. To enable still more words to be printed, the phrases you write can be separated by 4-point bullets—round black dots 4 points in diameter. This eliminates punctuation marks and space between adjacent phrases.

To the right of this copy block an arrow leads the eye from the price to the request for action—"Don't Delay—Order Today." To the right of this is a further inducement to ordering: a special free bonus offer of a complete set of blank business forms will be included at no extra cost if the customer orders the book within ten days. A free offer of something of real value to the customer but which costs the advertiser very little is of great help in selling the product or service, and in getting orders returned with little delay. Always try to make such an offer. It will build profits fast.

The remaining four blocks of copy on side 3 are set off with attention-getting headlines. Each headline picks out a strong selling point with basic emotional appeal and supports it with a few lines of copy. Each block either states or implies that many more details will be found in the book, thus assisting in convincing the reader to send in an order.

Note that these four copy blocks, two small and two larger, are set asymmetrically so that the headlines break up the blocks of solid type and contribute to a more pleasing appearance.

SIDE 4

Side 4 of the sample folder has a much smaller but equally important job to do. This is the place for your guarantee and for a final pitch to the reader to order right now. And you will remind him once again of the special free bonus offer for placing his order right away. Figure 9-2 illustrates the treatment suggested for side 4.

The guarantee is enclosed in a standard border which most printers have in stock. The headline above the guarantee makes a selling point and proclaims both your honesty and the value of your product to the customer.

The left half of side 4 includes two standard line illustrations which imply wealth and leisure. The headline promises success and all that implies to the reader. The text in the copy block will be a compelling pitch to the customer, and the display type at the bottom—"Order Your Copy Today"—reiterates the request for action.

METHODS OF COPY FITTING

Two things are involved in writing the copy for your mailing pieces: (1) saying what you want to say and (2) saying it in the space available. The number of words you can put on your folder depends upon the folder's size, on how much space is allotted to copy vs. space for headlines and art, and on the size of type you choose.

You have already drawn your layout and sketched in your headlines, so you know how much space you have left for copy. To get a rough idea as to how many words to write to fit the space, use one of the methods described below. All of these methods depend upon your knowing the size type and leading you want to use. (Type size and selection is discussed in chapter 8.)

To estimate length of copy, you will also need a ruler or a pica rule. The pica is the standard unit used by all typesetters and printers to measure type and space, and pica rules can be purchased at graphic art supply stores, or your printer may know where to get one.

WORDS PER SQUARE INCH

One way to get an idea of how many words will fill each copy block is to calculate the number of square inches in the block and multiply that figure by the number of words per square inch as shown in table 9-1. Table 9-1 shows *approximate* words per square inch depending upon type size and leading. A word is considered to have five letters.

TABLE 9–1 APPROXIMATE WORDS PER SQUARE INCH

	Words Per Square Inch		
Type Size	Set Solid	1 Point Leading	2 Points Leading
5½ point	70	60	50
6 point	50	45	36
7 point	36	32	29
8 point	28	24	23
9 point	23	20	19
10 point	18	18	16
11 point	16	14	14
12 point	13	11	11
14 point	9	9	9
18 point	7	7	7

Say your copy block is 3″ wide and 1½″ high, and you have selected 8-point type with 2 points leading. You would figure the number of words this way: 3″ x 1½″ = 4½ square inches in the copy block. Table 9-1 shows 23 words per square inch for 8-point type leaded 2 points. Multiply the number of square inches in the copy block by the number of words per square inch: 23 x 4½″ = 103½ words. Round this off to 104 words, and you have an approximate number of five-letter words that will fit your copy block.

PICAS PER AVERAGE WORD

Another method of estimating length of copy assumes that the average (five-letter) word set in 12-point type occupies 3 picas. For every 2 points of type size below 12-point type, deduct ½ pica from the 3 picas; for every 2 points above 12-point, add ½ pica. Using this method, an average word set in 8-point type will occupy 2 picas. If your copy block is 18 picas (3 inches) wide and each word occupies an average of 2 picas, then you can fit about 9 five-letter words on a line of type.

Now you know words per line. But how many lines will fit in your copy block? Refer to table 9-2, which shows lines of type per vertical inch for a variety of type sizes and leadings. Assuming the same 3″ x 1½″ copy block as in the previous example, set in 8-point type with 2 points leading, we see from table 9-2 that there will be about 11 lines of type in the block. Multiplying 9 words per line times 11 lines gives 99 words in the copy block.

TABLE 9–2 APPROXIMATE LINES OF TYPE PER VERTICAL INCH

	Lines Per Vertical Inch		
Type Size	Set Solid	1 Point Leading	2 Points Leading
5½ point	14	12	10
6 point	12	11	9
7 point	10	9	8
8 point	9	8	7
9 point	8	7	7
10 point	7	7	6
11 point	7	6	6
12 point	6	5	5
14 point	5	5	5
18 point	4	4	4

CHARACTERS PER PICA

The character count method of copy fitting is somewhat more accurate than the methods described above. Table 9-3 shows the average number of characters (letters, numbers, *punctuation marks, and spaces*) per pica of common typefaces used to set body copy. To figure the number of characters per line of type in a copy block, simply multiply the number of characters per pica by the number of picas in the width of the block. Thus a copy block 18 picas wide will contain 18 x 3.2 or about 57 characters per line of 8-point type. Set up your typewriter to type this number of characters per line. How many lines to type to fill the block can be figured from table 9-2.

The actual characters per pica for a typeface can vary from the average depending upon the style of typeface, the method of typesetting, number of capital letters in the copy, and so on. Your typesetter will probably be able to tell you characters per pica for the specific typeface you want. If not, the average figures shown in table 9-3 will be adequate for estimating the length of copy to write.

CHARACTERS PER INCH

Using table 9-4, you can figure out how many characters will be in each line of type by multiplying the number of characters per inch by the width of your copy area. For example, using 8-point type again, we find it gives 19 characters per inch. For a 3″ wide copy block, this will give 19 x 3 or 57 characters per line. Now you can set up your typewriter to type 57 characters per line, and refer to table 9-2 for the number of lines to type to fill your copy block.

| TABLE 9–3 | | TABLE 9–4 | |
| AVERAGE CHARACTERS PER PICA | | APPROXIMATE CHARACTERS PER INCH | |
Type Size	Characters Per Pica	Type Size	Characters Per Inch
6 point	4.2	5½ point	32
7 point	3.6	6 point	25
8 point	3.2	7 point	22
9 point	2.8	8 point	19
10 point	2.6	9 point	17
11 point	2.3	10 point	16
12 point	2.1	11 point	14
14 point	1.8	12 point	13
		14 point	11
		18 point	9

The above methods for approximating the number of words needed to fill a copy area will provide you with just that—an approximation. Depending upon the exact typeface chosen, the number of capital letters in your copy, how the type is set, and so on, your typeset copy may be a line or two shorter or longer than you estimated. It may even be off by several lines if you have a lot of copy. Your folder should be designed to accommodate these differences. Don't design your layout so tightly that great problems will occur if the typeset copy is a bit shorter or longer than estimated.

ESTIMATING SPACE NEEDED FOR COPY

The procedures outlined above showed you how to determine the number of words needed to fill a certain amount of space. But what about the reverse? What if you have your copy written and want to figure out how much space to allow for it on your layout? First count the number of words in the copy. Then decide on the type size and leading. Refer to table 9-1 and determine the average number of words per square inch for that size type and leading. Now divide the number of words in the copy by the number of words per square inch obtained from table 9-1. The result is the number of square inches of space needed to accommodate the copy.

For example, say you have written 135 words, and you want to set it in 10-point type with 1 point leading. Table 9-1 shows 18 words per square inch. Dividing 135 by 18 gives 7½ square inches. This is how much space you must allow on the folder for the copy.

ADJUSTING TYPE SIZE

Often you will write copy and be faced with fitting it in a particular space. For example, what if, in the previous situation, you only had 6 square inches space for 135 words of copy? You can often make copy fit the space by choosing a smaller type, less leading, or both. The reverse is also true—you can expand your copy to fill space by using a larger type size or more leading, or both.

First count the number of words in the copy. Then calculate the number of square inches available for it on your layout. Divide the number of words in the copy by the number of square inches of space. The result shows the number of words which must be printed in each square inch of copy block. If you had to fit 135 words in 6 square inches, you would divide 135 by 6 and come up with 22½ words per square inch. Now refer to table 9-1 to determine which size type will provide that number of words per square inch. According to the table, you could use 8-point type with 2 points leading, 9-point type set solid, or maybe you could get by with 9-point type with 1 point leading.

WRITING HARD-HITTING COPY

As you are composing the copy for your mailing pieces, you will probably have to type it over several times, making it tighter, giving it sparkle and emotional impact. If you have established the length of typed line you need to fit a certain space, be sure to average out over-runs with short lines as you type, as discussed in chapter 6.

In writing copy for your major sales pitch, type everything you can imagine that the product will do for the reader if he buys. *Use simple words and phrases*. In many cases, complete sentences are not desired since they add words without adding information and you have no room for words which are not working hard.

Polish and tighten your copy as often as necessary to get as many of the most important points into the fewest words. Keep in mind that the reader is mentally asking not only "What's in it for me?" but also "Will this product *really* do what the advertising says it will?"

Figure 9-4 is an example of a hard-hitting copy describing this book as the mail-order product. It answers the reader's silent question "Will this book *really* teach me *all* I'll need to know to be successful and earn more money?" This copy does exactly what you want it to do, and it is written to fit a particular space.

Businesses you can start on a shoestring •
Businesses which offer the greatest profits • Businesses which will grow bigger
fast • What makes the customer tick • How to
make people buy • How to find a sure-fire
product or service to sell • Reaching more
customers for less money • How to write
short classified ads which pull • How to
create mailing pieces that make people buy
from you • How to handle inquiries, orders
and money • Easy ways to cut costs • Best
times to advertise in newspapers and magazines for greatest profits • Easy ways to
expand your income with tie-in products

Fig. 9-4   Descriptive copy that sells.

Figure 9-5 shows another example of copy writing and fitting. Your copy might look like this after you have worked on it a bit. The numbers to the right of the copy block indicate how many letters short or long the line is. Notice how short lines balance over-runs so the lines average out to have the same number of characters each.

The copy answers the "What's in it for me?" question five different ways, all of which are strong selling points. The word *you* or *yours* appears 7 times in the 29 words used, approximately 25 percent, yet is not a blatant appeal. Any form of the word *you* helps establish a personal relationship between advertiser and reader and tends to instill confidence.

The copy is quite usable as written. But perhaps the copy can be tightened further. For example, it would be preferable to eliminate divided words at ends of lines to save space and make the copy look better. A bit more work on the copy and you probably will end up with something like that in figure 9-6.

Figure 9-6 is an even better piece of copy. It still stresses *you* or *yours* 7 times in 30 words. It answers the "What's in it for me?" question six different ways, one more than in the previous copy example. It urges action as it increases interest. It is simply worded. All divided words have been eliminated. There is no waste; every word is working hard. It adequately fills the space for the copy block. If used on the front of a folder, the impact of this copy will practically force the reader, guided by an arrowhead beneath it, to open the folder and be exposed to your major sales appeal.

Note the use of all capital letters in two words—YOU and NOW. This adds emphasis to your message, and urgency is also implied by use of exclamation points in two places at the ends of lines of type. Such emphasis should be used sparingly. Too much use of exclamation points and other tricks with copy and it loses its desired effect.

GETTING YOUR COPY TYPESET

Once you have written copy and headlines to fit your needs, neatly mark on each section of copy and on your layout the type size you want the copy set in. The shorthand way to do this is to write 8/9 for 8-point type with 1 point leading, 8/10 for 8-point type with 2 points leading, 9/10 for 9-point type with 1 point leading, etc. If you know what typeface you want, such as Times Roman or Helvetica, write that down, too. Take the copy to your job printer if he sets type, or to a local typesetter recommended by your printer. As described in the previous chapter, the printer or typesetter can help you select specific typefaces for body copy and display heads according to what they have available. Tell him you want reproduction proofs to use to make your own mechanicals, and ask for at least two sets of proofs. Ask when the proofs will be ready.

```
You will be          -2        You are your own      0
your own boss. Work  +3        boss. Work only      -1
when YOU feel like   +2        when YOU want to!    +1
it.  Your custom-    +1        Money for you in      0
ers will send        -3        every mail. No       -2
their money to you.  +3        selling required.    +1
No selling neces-    +1        Your home is your    +1
sary. Your home      -1        office. Success      -1
is your office.      -1        can be yours NOW!    +1
```

Fig. 9–5   Good sales copy that fits the space (left).
Fig. 9–6   Better sales copy that better fits the space (right).

When you pick up the proofs, be sure you get all pages of your original copy. Take them home and proofread the proofs. Proofreading means reading and comparing your original copy with the typeset copy. This is done to make certain that there are no misspelled words or other errors in the typeset copy. Of course, the typesetter cannot be considered responsible if you have errors in your original copy. His job is to duplicate your copy, not to argue whether it is correct or not. This is *your* job, so be certain you do it well. Carefully read and be certain of every word in the copy you submit to the typesetter, and then carefully read the proofs against your original copy. If there are errors on the proof, have them corrected and get two sets of corrected proofs.

LINE ART

If you want to have illustrations on your mailing piece, you have two choices: line art or photographs. Line art is the least expensive to use and will be discussed first.

Line art is any one-color line drawing, such as a pen and ink sketch. Line illustrations can be very effective on your mailing pieces and there are several sources for them. If you have the talent, you can draw illustrations yourself, or have an artistic friend draw them. This way your drawings will be original and distinctive. Another source is your printer. He frequently will have numerous pieces of clip art, or small line drawings, for you to choose from. Clip art is also provided in books which you can buy and use without being concerned with copyright since the price of these books includes royalties and fees. These books can be found at art supply stores.

Yet another source of illustrations and ornaments are sheets of transfer art, available at art supply stores. The ornaments can be positioned and rubbed in place on the mechanical with a *burnisher* (a small plastic wedge), or with a ballpoint pen or spoon handle.

Similar to transfer art are sheets of plastic film with shading patterns and symbols such as arrowheads of all sizes and shapes, circles, stars, comets, figures of automobiles, planes and ships, male and female figures, and house outlines. These patterns and ornaments are available in brands such as Zip-a-Tone, and they can be very helpful in making up mechanicals for your advertising materials. Note the two arrows used in the layout of figures 9-2 and 9-3, the border around the guarantee, and the small pieces of line art used. Most of these are available on plastic film.

The shading patterns can be especially effective in introducing shadows and giving the appearance of form and solidity to a two-dimensional drawing. Line art can, of course, be shaded by hand to give it depth and texture, but this requires some artistic ability. It is much easier to use one or more of the shading patterns. Dots, parallel lines, cross-hatching, and numerous other patterns are available in white, black, and in varying densities. Although shading film is fairly expensive, it will last a long time because you will use very little of it at one time. It is simple to apply and can produce very effective results when properly used.

To apply this type of film for shading, detach it from its backing sheet and lay it *gently* over the drawing to be shaded. Smooth it down over the shaded areas very softly, using the fleshy tip of your finger. Cut through the film with an X-Acto knife around the area to be shaded. Be very careful not to cut through the line drawing. Lift the excess film carefully by one corner, leaving the cut-out portion adhering to the drawing. Replace the unused film on its backing sheet. On the drawing, burnish the shading film down with the back of a fingernail or a burnisher.

If your line art is the right size, it can be placed in position on your mechanical to be photographed right along with the type in the plate-making process. If the art must be made smaller or larger to fit your layout, it should be mounted on a separate piece of cardboard and scaled to size (marked for reduction or enlargement). Sizing art is discussed in greater detail in the next section on photographs.

PHOTOGRAPHS

Photographs are quite costly to have printed in your advertising. They should be avoided if a line drawing can be used with equal effect.

Using a photograph requires making an extra negative and stripping it into the line negative (the negative made from photographing your mechanical with the typeset copy on it). It also necessitates that a photographic print be made if you make any modifications on the photograph itself. Since this is frequently necessary, your costs will increase in proportion. If you are incapable of making the necessary modifications on the face of the photograph, you will have to pay for the services of an illustrator or graphic retouch artist. For these reasons, photographs should be avoided if it is possible to do without them. Later when your business grows sufficiently the additional costs can be painlessly absorbed.

If a photograph is required, have the picture taken by a professional industrial photographer. He should be experienced in photographing items similar to the one you are selling. If possible, the photographer should do his own developing, enlarging, and printing rather than sending this work out to a commercial laboratory.

Always order two glossy prints (glossies) (plus one matte or dull finish print if you expect alterations will be necessary) 5" x 7" in size on single weight paper. The total photography cost should be between $25 and $50.

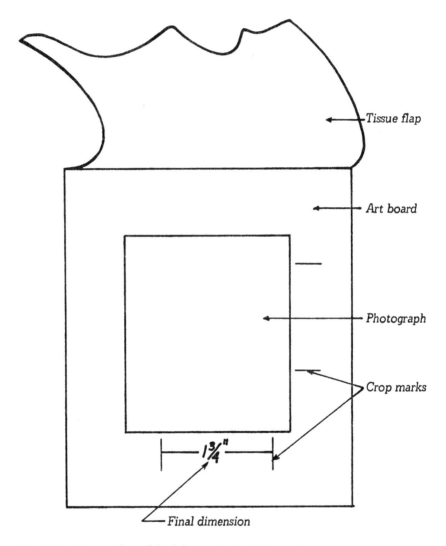

Fig. 9–7 Crop marks and final dimension for photograph.

Be sure the negative is returned to you for filing unless the photographer retains ownership of all negatives he shoots. Check with the photographer for his policy on negatives before contracting with him for any work.

Retain one glossy print in your files for possible future use. (It costs less than $5 and is well worth it.) The matte print has a soft, rough finish which will take pencil and pen markings if necessary. Coat the back of the remaining glossy print with rubber cement and attach it to a piece of bristol board. This is the one you will send to the printer. Protect the face of the photograph with a piece of tissue paper taped to the back and folded over to cover the photo.

Your 5" x 7" photograph is larger than your want on your mailing piece and probably has a lot of space around the subject of the picture. You will want to *crop* the extra space and indicate how small to print the picture. Determine how much of the area of the photograph is to appear in print and draw ink crop marks on the surface of the bristol board. Write in the *final size width* (the width you want the printed picture to be) between the appropriate set of crop marks (see figure 9-7).

Now replace the tissue flap over the photograph and temporarily insert beneath it a sheet of transparent, stiff acetate (sheet plastic). With a soft pencil lightly trace the rectangular area you want to reproduce and draw a line diagonally across this rectangle from the upper right corner to the lower left corner. Measure the *final size width* of the photograph along the bottom of the outline, starting from the lower left-hand corner. Draw a vertical line to the diagonal line at this point, using T-square and triangle, and a horizontal line from this intersection to the left margin of the outline. See figure 9-8. This smaller rectangle is the same size and shape as the photograph will be when reduced and printed.

If the background of the photograph is to be removed, this can be done in either of two ways. Outline the desired area very carefully with white poster paint to a width of at least ¼ inch. Or, using your X-Acto knife, with extreme care cut around the object in the photograph and carefully peel off the unwanted surrounding areas. Removing the background can be tricky—one careless mistake and you may damage the artwork. Since you are going to the expense of putting a photograph in your mailing piece, it may be better to let a professional handle this. Your photographer or printer can advise you.

Arrows and leaders (lines without arrowheads) are easy to apply to photographs when it is desired to point out specific features to the reader. Such items are available in sheets, as described above under line art, and individual arrows can be cut and burnished down on the photograph. They have a waxed or adhesive backing and stick well but can be lifted should this be necessary.

Your mounted, cropped and scaled art is now ready to send out with your mechanical for printing.

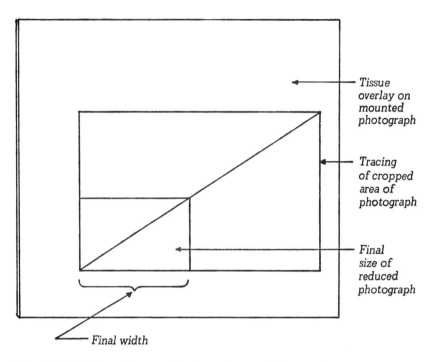

Fig. 9–8   Marking a tissue overlay for reduction of photograph.

CREATING YOUR MECHANICAL

A mechanical is simply the original from which the offset plate is eventually made. It looks identical to each unfolded page of your final mailing piece except that it consists, mechanically, of a large piece of cardboard upon which you have pasted typeset display heads, copy blocks, and line art in the places you wish them to appear on the final printed page. These display heads and copy blocks are cut from the proofs you had made.

Our sample single-fold folder will require two mechanicals—one for sides 1 and 4 and one for sides 2 and 3. Your original layout is your guide for pasting up the mechanical. You will want to have your line illustrations, if any, selected and on hand for use on the mechanical.

Supplies

There are a minimum number of tools and supplies which you will need to produce a professional mechanical. These are listed below.

X-Acto knife or single-edge razor blades
No. 11 blades for X-Acto knife, if used
Drawing board 15″ x 24″ or larger

T-square, 24″ long or longer
Thumb tacks
Masking tape
Plastic triangle, 12″, 30°–60°–90°
Bristol or art board, 1/16″ thick or thicker
Bottle of rubber cement with brush
Rubber cement thinner (flammable)
Eagle Veri-Thin No. 240½ pencil, sky blue
Pen and ink
Ruler or pica rule, 24″ long
Tissue paper
Sno-Pake, White-Out, Liquid Paper, or other white opaquing fluid
Thinner for white opaquing fluid
Art gum eraser
Pink Pearl eraser, or equivalent

You will use practically all of these each time you make up a mechanical. Since they are relatively inexpensive you should buy them. Any average-quality drawing board, T-square, and triangle will be adequate; you will not need the most expensive ones.

There is one item in this list for which, to the author's knowledge, there is no substitute. This is the Eagle Veri-Thin No. 240½ Sky Blue nonreproducible pencil. They may be difficult to locate, although a graphic arts supply house or office supply store should have them. If they are scarce, buy a dozen. If you can't find any to purchase, ask printers, advertising agencies, and industrial photographers. They will probably give you one or at least tell you where you can buy them. This pencil is indispensable because it makes a light blue mark which will not be reproduced by the camera when your mechanical is photographed. Any other color is usually picked up on the film. If you use this pencil to draw light lines to establish the positions of your copy blocks, headlines, and art, they need not be erased. Likewise, if you keep the white surface of the mechanical reasonably clean, minor smudges will not be picked up by the camera.

A razor blade can be used instead of the X-Acto knife but the knife is preferred and much easier to use. The No. 11 blades are triangular with extremely sharp points. The knife is used to cut apart your proofs. Pieces of copy may then be picked up on the point of the knife and positioned correctly on your mechanical.

MAKING THE MECHANICAL

1. The bristol or art board is the base for your mechanical. It should be large enough to have generous margins on all sides of the reproducible area (the area in which you will paste the copy blocks in place). Thumb tack or tape the board to the drawing board, lining it up with the

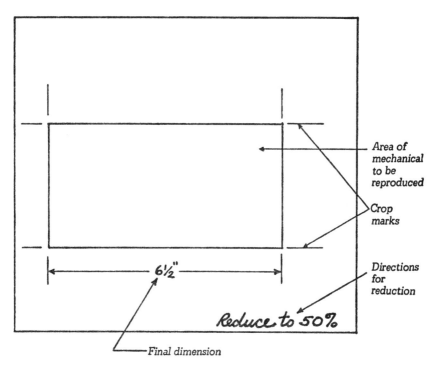

Area of
mechanical
to be
reproduced

Crop
marks

Directions
for
reduction

6½"

Reduce to 50%

Final dimension

Fig. 9–9   Crop marks on the mechanical. This mechanical is also marked for reduction.

T-square. With the nonreproducible pencil, T-square, and triangle, draw light lines indicating the margins of the reproducible area

2. When the outline is drawn, *outside* the reproducible area on the mechanical but *exactly* even with all four margins, draw short crop lines at each corner with pen and ink. Your crop marks will look something like those in figure 9-9. Crop marks indicate to the camera operator and the printer the exact area which you intend to be reproduced. Nothing outside the area indicated by these crop marks will appear in the final printed mailing piece.

3. With your layout as a guide and using T-square, triangle, and the light blue nonreproducible pencil, mark the surface of the board inside the margin lines *lightly* to show the exact position of all blocks of copy, drawings, and the *bottom* of each line of display type used for headlines.

4. When your guidelines are drawn, cut your proofs apart with the knife or razor blade, leaving ⅛ inch or more of margin outside the actual type or art. Position all separate pieces on your mechanical as you have laid it out. Make any adjustments necessary, erasing and redrawing the light blue guidelines as required. When you are completely satisfied with the appearance of the copy on your mechanical, remove all the separate pieces of proof.

5. Open your bottle of rubber cement. It will be somewhat thicker than desired. Pour about two tablespoons of the cement out on a separate piece of bristol board or other clean, hard surface. Smear the cement out thinly and let it dry. You will rub it up later and use it to clean your mechanical. While this cement is drying, add some thinner to your bottle of rubber cement and mix it well. When it is well mixed, cover the entire surface of your bristol board inside the margin lines with a thin coating of rubber cement. Be thorough, but spread the cement thinly. Don't worry about smearing it somewhat outside the margin. It will be easy to remove later.

6. Allow the cement to dry. Turn all pieces of proof copy needed for the mechanical face down on a clean, dry surface. Lightly coat the backs with rubber cement and allow it to dry. Be sure not to allow any two surfaces coated with rubber cement to touch each other. They will immediately stick together and may be damaged if pulled apart.

7. Now lay a sheet of tissue paper (you can also use ordinary waxed paper) over the surface of your mechanical. Turn the individual pieces of proof copy over on a clean, dry surface. Slide the tissue or wax paper down to expose an area where one piece of copy, a headline for instance, will be placed. Pick up the appropriate piece of copy with the knife point, or with your fingers, making certain not to touch the printed surface. Position it *gently* in place, *very lightly*, adjusting its position with the knife until it is exactly where it belongs; then lightly press it in place with the knife.

8. Continue as described above until all copy elements and line illustrations are in the positions they are to occupy. Minor adjustments can still be made with the knife. If any pieces must be removed and repositioned, recoat the mechanical and the back of the fresh piece of copy with rubber cement and allow both to dry. If a piece of copy is smudged or torn, replace it with the same copy from another of your proof copies. (This is the main reason for having several copies of proofs pulled.)

To indicate position of photographs or line art that are mounted on separate boards, simply outline the area on the mechanical *lightly* with your blue nonreproducible pencil and write the word "photo" or "figure" in the box. If your mailing piece has more than one piece of art, be sure to number the art and key it to the appropriate space.

9. When the mechanical is in its final form, lay the tissue or waxed paper over the surface and burnish each copy element in place by firmly rubbing over the tissue or wax paper with a fingernail, toothbrush handle, or a burnishing tool; then remove the tissue or waxed paper.

10. To clean the mechanical, return to the two spoonsful of rubber cement smeared on the clean board. It will be dry by now. With your fingers, roll the dried cement onto itself, forming an unattractive wad. Note that the spare board shows no evidence of ever having had rubber

cement applied to it. This is the reason that rubber cement is so useful in the graphic arts. It is clean, easy to use, and simple to remove. With your wad of dried rubber cement, lightly rub over exposed cement-covered portions of your mechanical to pick up the leftover cement. Do not rub over the pasted-down type or you may smear it since the ink never dries completely on a slick surface.

11. When the excess rubber cement has been removed from your mechanical, remove any dirt or smudges with an art gum eraser or cover them with the white opaquing fluid. *Carefully* go over the edges of each piece of pasted-down copy with this white opaque. This eliminates shadows cast by the edges of the thicker portions of copy from photographing as lines.

When you have completed treating the edges of each copy element, you may feel the entire thing looks messy and not very professional. The camera cannot "see" the white opaque, and because you have covered the edges of all copy elements, the camera will also not "see" the edges as shadow lines. Don't concern yourself with what it looks like to *you;* you have only to make sure it looks right to the camera—and it will if you have followed these directions carefully.

12. To protect the mechanical, cut a length of tissue paper the same width as the board and two inches longer than its height. Lay the board face down on the tissue with the excess tissue extending above the top of the board. Fold this flap over the back of the board and hold it in place with masking tape. This tissue overlay protects the surface from being soiled or damaged. The manner in which it is attached makes it easy for the camera operator to place it out of the way while it is being photographed.

13. If you have made your mechanical in exactly the same size in which you want it printed, write the words "Same Size" in the lower margin on the front of the board, outside the crop marks. (Oversize mechanicals are discussed in the next section.) The mechanical should also be marked on the back with the name, address, and telephone number of your company. In addition, it should be marked with the date, the number of pieces to be printed, and a label describing what the printed pieces are and their intended use.

OVERSIZE MECHANICALS

The previous discussion on selecting type, getting the copy set, and pasting it up on a board has resulted in a mechanical that is the same size as your finished printed piece. But there are two big advantages to making your mechanical and its copy elements oversized, usually twice or four times the size of the actual printed piece. An oversize mechanical is easier to lay out and construct because copy elements are larger and there is plenty of space between them. In addition, the camera will automatically sharpen up the overall appearance, smooth any rough edges, and reduce angular errors as it reduces copy to final size. This makes for a much better-looking printing job than if the mechanical is made in final size and not reduced before printing.

To make an oversize mechanical, a ratio of two to one is recommended. This means that the light blue guidelines you draw on your mechanical will be twice as far apart as they would be if the mechanical were the same size as the final printed mailing piece. The oversize mechanical will be reduced in size by the camera so the offset plate will show the copy in the actual size to be printed. This means that on the mechanical *the size of all type and the dimensions of all copy elements, including artwork, must be double the final size*. Six-point type in the final must be set in 12-point size for pasting on the mechanical; a copy block two inches wide in the final size must be laid out four inches wide on the mechanical, etc.

An oversize mechanical will have to be marked so that the camera operator will know exactly how much to reduce it. If the mechanical is twice size, that is, twice the height and twice the width of the final printed piece, write "reduce to 50%" in the lower margin of the front of the board outside the crop marks. This tells the camera operator to adjust his camera so the image on the negative will be half the width and half the height of the area indicated by the crop marks. Reduce to 66% means to reduce the height or width (it doesn't matter which—the result will be the same) to two-thirds of the original. Remember to mark for reduction *to* the desired size, not *by* a specific amount.

Another method of marking copy for reduction is to mark one side between crop marks with the final dimension in inches, adding arrows as shown in figure 9-9. Either the height or width may be marked.

GETTING IT PRINTED

Your mechanicals and artwork are now ready to be taken to your printer. He will photograph the mechanicals, make the plates, and print your mailing pieces according to the specifications you and he discuss. Your printer can be one of your best advisers as to choice of paper and inks (these topics are discussed in the previous chapter).

Be sure you know how many copies you want printed, and whether or not you expect to print the same piece again. This will affect the type of plate that is made. Tell your printer you want to keep the negative. (Some job printers will own the negative and store it for you.) If you own the negative, store it carefully in an envelope, lying flat, to be used for future printings. If small corrections must be made on it, have them set, photographed, and stripped into the negative. Be sure, too, to save your layout with the sizes and styles of type marked on it. You will want it for future reference.

10

Equipment, Files, Records, and Forms

OFFICE EQUIPMENT AND SUPPLIES

Every business, even the smallest, needs at least some items of office equipment. Usually you will be able to purchase used office equipment, often for very little money. It is not necessary nor even desirable to attempt to furnish an office to rival that of the president—even if you are president of your own company and chairman of its board of directors. So forget about fancy mahogany desks, thick carpets, intercoms, push-button telephones, and small computers. At this stage you won't need walls of filing cabinets, original oil paintings, nor your own executive washroom. Put such grandiose thoughts into the back of your mind until your gross sales approach or exceed $50,000 a year. You will be able to pamper yourself then without hurting your business.

Do you need a *desk?* Possibly, although a sturdy table will do a good job for you and it will be a lot cheaper. Your mail order customers never see your office. Their impression of your business is gained through your advertising and your product or service, not the furniture in your office.

A *chair?* Certainly. But not a fancy swivel chair. You will use a chair to do some of your work so it should be a reasonably comfortable one. An ordinary kitchen chair with a cushioned seat will do at first. However, as soon as you can afford it, buy a second-hand *typist's chair*. It is comfortably padded, has no arm rests to get in the way, is adjustable in height, and has a scientifically designed back rest to reduce fatigue. It rolls on casters as well as swivels.

Filing cabinets? One will be needed eventually. Try to locate a second-hand, four-drawer letter size file cabinet. It need not have a lock.

One cabinet will last for quite awhile before you will really feel the need for another one.

Typewriter? Absolutely necessary, even if you're only a one-finger typist. Used typewriters are available from about $25 up. You don't need the latest electric model. A manual typewriter, properly maintained, will last a lifetime. An office machine will usually be more satisfactory than a portable, especially if only American-made typewriters are considered. With the spread in acceptance of electric typewriters in the business world you should be able to find a bargain in a used Royal, Underwood, or Smith-Corona typewriter.

Don't neglect foreign brands of typewriters as long as they have a standard keyboard with either pica or elite type. They are generally soundly constructed and high in quality. Consider Adler (German), Facit (Swedish), and Hermes (Swiss), among others. In the author's estimation there is no higher quality manual typewriter made in the world today than the Hermes. Both portable and office machines are available. The price may seem high (the price includes the import tariff as well as shipment from the factory in Switzerland), but if you can afford it, it's worth it.

Card files? Very necessary to keep track of inquiries and orders, and to build a valuable mailing list. File cards 3" x 5" are large enough. The small file boxes available for these cards are a nuisance, and the special metal cabinets fairly expensive, although they will never wear out. If you can find a two-drawer or larger card file cabinet used, at a price you can afford, buy it. However, you can use shoe boxes or build wooden trays which will serve the purpose adequately.

Postage scale? Yes, absolutely. It should be purchased new at an office supply store and be capable of accurately weighing to eight ounces or a pound, calibrated in ounces and fractions of an ounce. A scale enables you to eliminate waste of postage and to adjust each mailing to take advantage of postal regulations to get the most advertising into the hands of the customer at the lowest mailing cost.

If you sell a product which weighs more when packed than the capacity of your scale, you need not purchase additional scales. Have the first few packages weighed at the post office and make a note of the maximum weight. Use this weight as a guide to the amount of postage required for later shipments, as long as your method of packing and the materials used do not drastically change. Remember also that United Parcel Service is fast, efficient, and cheaper than the U.S. Postal Service in those states which enjoy this service. This can save you money in shipping your product to your customers.

Typewriter stand? Possibly. The best height above the floor for a typing table is 29 inches; most desks and tables are 31 inches high. If you use a secondhand typist's or secretary's desk with a special niche in one side for your typewriter you don't need a stand. Typewriter stands are rarely sufficiently sturdy and the really good ones tend to be expensive, even secondhand. An extension can be constructed at the end of your work table for your typewriter, using plywood and two-by-fours if you are a bit handy at carpentry.

A *work table* or *mailing table?* You'll need one several feet long. A cheaper and probably better substitute can be built as a wide shelf attached to the wall at waist height so you can work standing up, or sitting on a tall stool similar to a bar stool. A piece of three-quarter inch fir plywood two feet wide and eight feet long (half a standard sheet) will make an ideal work table when built in against one wall.

Book case? Why not shelves built along a wall? Not so much for books but for orderly storage of printed forms, stationery, envelopes, advertising mailing pieces, and perhaps stock. Shelves are handy for storage of cartons if you mail out your own product.

Rubber stamps? Yes. There are several stamps you should have. Check the listing below. Most will be useful regardless of your product or service, but get only those you know you will need.

    Date stamp, adjustable.
    Name, address, telephone number of your company.
    BOOKS—SPECIAL FOURTH CLASS RATE
    FIRST CLASS MAIL
    RETURN POSTAGE GUARANTEED
    FOR DEPOSIT ONLY. ACCOUNT NO._____(Company name
       and address; name of bank)
    FORWARDING POSTAGE GUARANTEED
    ORDER FILLED_____SHIPPED_____BY_____
    THANK YOU FOR YOUR ORDER
    REFUND CHECK
    PLEASE! PAST DUE

Adding machine or *calculator?* Yes, even if you feel you are an expert mathematician. Your figures have to be accurate. Electronic calculators with four functions (addition, subtraction, multiplication, and division) and a six- or eight-figure display and floating decimal point are available from about $10 up. You do not need functions such as memory key, percentage, square root, etc. Buy just the capabilities you need. Don't pay for features you will seldom or never use. Mechanical adding machines also are available at low secondhand prices, but your best buy will be a pocket-size, battery-operated four-function calculator.

Postage meter? Eventually, but not at the beginning. A postage meter will speed up your mailing when your volume reaches over 100 per day average. Below this figure, use postage stamps.

The items of equipment discussed above represent the major ones needed by every small mail order business. In addition to office equipment there are a number of other items which can be lumped under the heading of *office supplies*. These are available at office supply and variety stores. Purchase what you need but don't go overboard.

Many of the following items and supplies will be needed almost every day:

Stapler and staples
Staple remover
Stamp pads and ink
Pencils and pencil sharpener
Erasers
Ball point pens and refills
Calendars
Paper clips
3" x 5" file cards
Address labels, gummed on perforated sheets
Manila folders, letter size
Carbon paper or film
Index tabs
Labels for file folders
Cellophane tape
Stamp moistener
Fingertips
Canary bond (for carbon copies and scratch paper)
Library paste or white glue
Rubber cement and thinner (Caution! It's flammable!)
No. 11 blades for X-Acto knife (other blade shapes are available but
    No. 11 is best)
Zip-A-Tone, Craftint, or other film
Shipping cartons or bags
Shipping tape, gummed; or fiber tape, adhesive
Shipping labels (may be prepared by your printer)
Rubber bands
Memo pads
Ruled canary tablets
Letter opener
Deposit slips (free from your bank)
Typewriter ribbons
Typewriter error correction fluid or tape
Type cleaner (for typewriter)

SETTING UP FILES AND FINANCIAL RECORDS

Files are of extreme importance to every business and they must be kept, no matter how small your business is at the start. All files described in this book are valuable and are necessary to the control and operation of your business. For a typical mail order company, files must be established for the following classifications:

1. Inquiries
2. Orders
3. Correspondence
4. Advertising effectivity
5. Business expenses and tax records

INQUIRY AND ORDER FILES

All inquiries you receive are valuable even though not all will result in orders. The names and addresses of all who write to you are valuable as a mailing list, both those who buy and those who don't. Three separate card files are necessary to control these names and addresses from the initial inquiry to the final completed order (or lack of order). These files are called Pending, Tickler, and Completed.

Pending File—set up the Pending File alphabetically according to the initial letter of each person's last name. Each file card contains a pasted-on label with the name and address of the person who replied to your ad, the date, and the code key of the advertisement answered or the name of the publication in which the ad appeared. Attached to the file card with a paper clip is one gummed address label. The card is not filed until your follow-up advertising has been addressed and is ready for mailing. The cards in the Pending File will be referred to when an order is received, or after 30 days have elapsed without an order coming in.

Tickler File—Set up this card file numerically with card separators numbered 1 through 30, corresponding to the numbered days of the month. In months having 31 days, this extra day is considered as being the 30th day. Into this file under today's date goes a file card which is a duplicate copy of the card in the Pending File, with one address label clipped to it and only the name and address typed on the label that is pasted on the card. The Tickler File controls the time that cards are allowed to remain dormant in the Pending File if no order is received. This allows you to mail another follow-up message (a second chance mailing) to each person who has not ordered from you within 30 days of the time you first replied to his inquiry. This second chance will bring in orders which might otherwise be lost. Exact procedures for utilizing the Tickler File, including a step-by-step chart, are presented in the next chapter.

Completed File—This card file is set up alphabetically in two sections, each covering the entire alphabet. Into the first section of the order file go the file cards from the Pending File when an order is received and shipped. Into the second section go the file cards from the Tickler File if no order has been received within 60 days after the initial inquiry, or 30 days after your second chance mailing was made, when the name can be considered "dead."

Each section of this file will eventually contain twin cards which were originally in the Pending and Tickler files, so each name will be represented by two cards. As they accumulate, you will be able to rent or sell these names to other companies who sell by direct mail, and even the names who did not order are valuable.

CORRESPONDENCE FILE

Set up a correspondence file in one drawer of your filing cabinet. Use a separator for each letter of the alphabet. File correspondence you intend to keep in alphabetical order in manila folders. You will have no need to file all the correspondence you get. Inquiries should be discarded *after* cards have been inserted in the Pending and Tickler files. The correspondence you will want to keep will be the letters from both satisfied and dissatisfied customers, together with copies of your replies, if any.

Unsolicited testimonial letters from satisfied customers can later be incorporated in your advertising as proof of the desirability of your product or service. Letters from disgruntled customers may provide hints to improve your advertising, product, or service, and show if a refund was made. This latter fact should be entered with the date on the margin of the letter. This constitutes a record for tax and postal inspectors should they wish to check your records. Your canceled checks, of course, are your primary tax records and corroborate the refund notations on the customer letters.

ADVERTISING FILES

Your advertising files will take two forms. A card file using 3″ x 5″ cards should be set up alphabetically, listing by name, address, and classified ad rate all periodicals in which you have placed or may eventually place advertising. The advertising deadline and month of publication versus the cover date of each should also be entered on these cards. The key used to identify each periodical should be noted at the upper left of the face of each card. A copy of the ad being run, clipped from each magazine, should be pasted on the back of each card. Also on the reverse side of each card is a list of date, check numbers, and amount spent with each periodical for advertising. A second card can be stapled to the first when its back becomes filled with information.

In the front of the file place a key card identifying each magazine or newspaper by the key used in each ad.

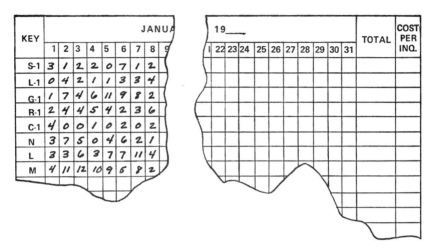

Fig. 10–1   Advertising returns chart.

The second part of your advertising file takes the form of a chart and can be hung on the wall if desired. It is set up as illustrated in figure 10-1. The chart is divided into 34 columns and as many rows as the number of different periodicals in which you advertise. The number of inquiries received as a result of ads in each month's periodical is entered on the chart each day and totaled each month on the right. This chart shows at a glance which periodicals are pulling and which are not. For each periodical the cost per inquiry (cost of ad for the month divided by the number of inquiries received) can be calculated and entered on the chart each month. This gives you a true picture of how much your advertising actually costs you and therefore how effective it is.

These charts should be saved for three year periods so you can make quick comparisons between years to determine how well your business is doing. Because only 12 sheets are needed each year, these files take up little storage space. A large pad of paper can be provided by your printer or you can buy newsprint sketch pads in various sizes at any art supply store. Either will be ideal for your purpose.

BUSINESS EXPENSES

Set aside a portion of one drawer in your filing cabinet for controlling your business expense records. Set up a separate manila folder for each of the following classifications *which applies to your business:*

  Advertising (classified and display ads)
  Photography (business related)
  Printing (business related)

Postage (all business mail of any kind)
Office supplies (expendables)
Office equipment maintenance (repair costs)
Capital equipment (for depreciation purposes)
Rent
Utilities (electricity, heat, water, sewer, trash)
Transportation (business related)
Entertainment (very doubtful in mail order)
Product research (samples, magazines, etc.)
Charity (contributions in the name of your company)
Insurance (business, stock, facilities)
Interest (paid on business loans)
Professional dues (pertaining to business)
Product inventory (stock)
Janitorial services and supplies
Technical books and subscriptions (business related)
Checking account service charges, check charges

All of the above, if they apply to your business, represent legitimate.costs of doing business and as such are legally deductible from business income for tax purposes. The manner and extent of deducting expenses such as rent, utilities, transportation, and business entertainment are subject to change at any time. You should check with an income tax expert or the Internal Revenue Service to determine current regulations at tax time each year.

In each of the folders described go receipts, canceled checks, and notes detailing deductible expenses. Keep cash payments to the absolute minimum and use your business checking account to pay bills and make purchases.

FINANCIAL RECORDS

For your financial records, set up twelve manila folders, one for each month. Into these place duplicate deposit slips showing income received from orders and deposited in your bank. At the end of each month add the totals of all money received (as listed on each deposit slip). This is your *gross income* for the month, and the total of the deposit slips in all folders is your gross income for the year.

From this *gross income* subtract all business expenses, some of which, like depreciation and some printing costs, will be distributed over a number of months or years. The result is your *net income* for the year, before taxes. This net income represents payment to you for your work and profits from your business, out of which income taxes must be paid.

Figure 10-2 illustrates a simple chart which may be used to calculate

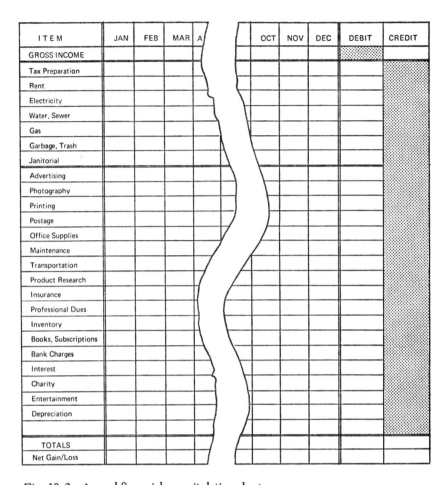

ITEM	JAN	FEB	MAR	A		OCT	NOV	DEC	DEBIT	CREDIT
GROSS INCOME										
Tax Preparation										
Rent										
Electricity										
Water, Sewer										
Gas										
Garbage, Trash										
Janitorial										
Advertising										
Photography										
Printing										
Postage										
Office Supplies										
Maintenance										
Transportation										
Product Research										
Insurance										
Professional Dues										
Inventory										
Books, Subscriptions										
Bank Charges										
Interest										
Charity										
Entertainment										
Depreciation										
TOTALS										
Net Gain/Loss										

Fig. 10–2   Annual financial recapitulation chart.

net gain or loss before taxes for the year. One such chart will be needed each year you are in business. The headings at the left side of the chart are the same headings that appear on your business expense files.

At the end of each month, enter the monthly income on this chart and add up the total amounts paid out for the month, using the receipts and canceled checks in each of the expense folders. Enter these totals on the chart and place each batch of receipts and canceled checks in an envelope. Seal the envelope, mark the month and type of expense (printing, rent, advertising) on each envelope, and return it to the proper folder.

You may, if you wish, determine net gain or loss each month on the chart. However, this will not give you a true picture of the status of your business except at the end of each year. Advertising paid for in one month will not bring in returns until several months in the future. Similarly, you will have to pay your major printing bills one, two, or three times a year. The months in which you pay this bill may show a loss, but it is not actually a loss since the printing paid for in one month will be used to obtain orders in many of the following months.

After your first year or two in business you *will* be able to determine your approximate financial status on a month-to-month basis. You will know how much money you spend each year for such items as printing, advertising, and postage. You can divide these totals by 12 to arrive at an average amount which can be prorated each month rather than listing these expenses when they are incurred.

Example: Suppose you order printing twice a year and pay $240 in March and $240 in September. Divide the total of $480 by 12, and the result represents an average (prorated) charge of only $40 a month for printing over the entire year. If the large, periodic expenses are handled in this way instead of listing them only in March and September, for example, it will give you much more accurate results in calculating net gain (income) each month.

A SIMPLE MONTHLY RECORD SYSTEM

One of the simplest methods of keeping track of income and expenses on a monthly basis is to use an order spike. This makes your use of the chart illustrated in figure 10-2 even easier. An order spike is a long, stiff, sharp wire mounted on a weighted base. It can be kept on your work table or mounted high on the wall.

Every time you deposit order checks and money, impale the duplicate deposit slip on the spike. Every time you pay a bill, place the duplicate bill or receipt on the spike. If you make any payment which does not result in a receipt, write the details on a slip of paper and put this on the spike. Thus an accurate record of income and expenses over a one-month period will gradually pile up on the spike.

At the end of the month, remove all papers from the spike and separate deposit slips from expense receipts. Add the deposits and enter the total for the month on the form as gross income. Then add the totals for each type of expense and enter these totals in the appropriate blanks. Place deposit slips and receipts in separate, marked and sealed envelopes, and insert them in the appropriate file folders.

INCOME VS. ADVERTISING COSTS

You will want to know how much actual net income derives from the classified advertising placed in each periodical you use. The results will

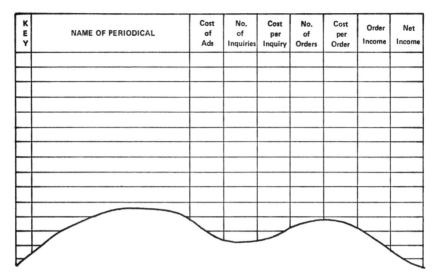

K E Y	NAME OF PERIODICAL	Cost of Ads	No. of Inquiries	Cost per Inquiry	No. of Orders	Cost per Order	Order Income	Net Income

Fig. 10–3   Income vs. advertising chart.

be valid over a year's time and will enable you to see which periodicals give you the most income *per dollar spent*. These results also point out periodicals· which are not sufficiently productive. You can thus consider dropping them in favor of others which may produce more real income.

Figure 10-3 illustrates a chart designed to pinpoint income from the ads in each periodical. The information required to fill in this chart is taken from the entries in figures 10-1 and 10-2, from the order section of your Completed File, and from your financial records in manila folders.

The chart shown in figure 10-3 is normally filled in once each year, usually around the anniversary of your first starting in business, although it can also be maintained on a calendar-year basis. Either method will give accurate results after you have been in business at least 12 months.

In each line of the income vs. advertising chart the following information, taken from records, is entered:

The key used for each periodical
Name of each periodical
Total spent on classified advertising for the past year
Number of inquiries received
Cost per inquiry (cost of ads divided by number of inquiries)
Number of orders received through each periodical
Cost per order (cost of ads divided by number of orders)
Income from orders through each periodical
Net income produced by each periodical

The cost per order is calculated by dividing the amount of money spent for advertising in the periodical by the number of keyed orders received through that periodical:

$$\text{Cost per order} = \frac{\text{Cost of advertisement}}{\text{Number of orders received}}$$

Net income is determined by subtracting the cost of advertising from total order income:

$$\text{Net income} = \text{Total order income} - \text{Cost of ad}$$

The net income is not always a good way to compare periodicals. In fact, the cost per order is the most useful item in determining whether your advertising budget is well spent. The cost per order shows you how much *in addition to the cost of your product or service and overhead expenses* must be deducted from the selling price to determine gross profit.

The lowest cost per order should be your goal, but do not completely ignore net income produced by the periodical. If it is low, perhaps the periodical does not reach an interested market. On the other hand, do not automatically eliminate a periodical which shows a high but acceptable cost per order as long as the net income is also acceptable. Remember that a dollar in profit after expenses is still a dollar in your pocket. The income vs. advertising chart is intended as a tool to increase your income from advertising. Don't let it become a shovel to bury you.

STATIONERY AND BUSINESS FORMS

Every business must have certain printed forms to conduct its day-to-day business. They need not be costly, but those adaptable to your specific product or service should be on hand and ready for use when needed. Your direct mail advertising materials, order blanks, return envelopes, etc. were discussed in chapter 7. The various printed forms described in this chapter are considered necessary to doing business efficiently and are in addition to those discussed earlier in this book.

Not all the printed materials to be discussed will be needed to operate every business. For instance, purchase orders are unnecessary in most service businesses and invoices will not be needed unless you sell on credit. They are included here in the interest of completeness. Choose only those which you need and ignore the remainder.

The forms illustrated in the following pages need not be used exactly as shown. Both the design and the wording are necessarily general so that they apply to as many different businesses as possible. If they are not exactly what you need, do not hesitate to change them or to design your own special forms which suit your specific product or service.

In no case has typeface or size been specified. This must be your own decision, made in consideration of suggestions by your printer. Office supply stores have certain stock forms available which need only your company's name, address, and telephone number printed on them to make them yours. Inspect these stock forms and check their prices (plus what your printer will charge to add your imprint) before making up your mind. In most cases stock forms will be adequate and cheaper than having your own forms printed.

Business Card

You should have a business card. You will be dealing with local printers and other suppliers and an exchange of business cards is customary. They will keep your card on file. You should also maintain a file of suppliers' business cards. Small metal files for business cards, looking much like a card file, are available at most office supply stores. Some businesses give these files away free as advertising novelties.

Since your business card represents you not only as an executive but as a buyer of supplies and services, it should be neat and in good taste. A typical card design is illustrated in figure 10-4.

Business cards can be expensive. While it is always good community relations to have all your printing done locally, you may wish to order your business cards from a mail order source which gives you high-quality, fast, cheap service for 1000 business cards delivered to your door. Local prices for the same quantity and quality may be two or three times as costly. Dealers and job printers of business cards, envelopes, and

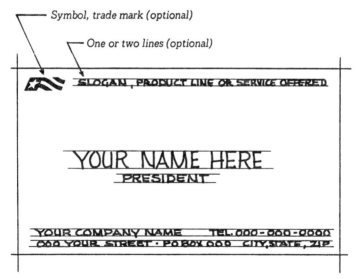

Fig. 10–4   Business card.

letterheads advertise constantly in the classified columns of such magazines as *Popular Mechanics, Science and Mechanics, Mechanix Illustrated,* and others. All provide samples and allow considerable latitude in the choice of type and wording.

It is customary for the business card of an executive to have his name in large type in the center, with his title in smaller type immediately below. The name, address, and telephone number of his company appear in small type across the bottom. A trade mark or logo, if you have designed one, can also appear on the card, usually in conjunction with the company name or at the upper left of the card. A line or two of additional information, *if really necessary,* can appear across the top of the card in small type.

Note that on the card illustrated in figure 10-4 both a street address and a post office box number appear. This is customary if you use a P.O. box number for a business address, but it is not necessary to have both addresses on your card unless you so desire. Either will suffice.

Your title will probably be either president or general manager, or possibly *president and general manager.* The choice is yours, though the last sounds a bit grandiose. One of the first two given here would be best and customary.

ENVELOPE

You may use either a No. 9 Official (3⅞" x 8⅞") or a No. 10 Official (4½" x 9½") envelope. The No. 9 is less costly. A folded 8½" x 11" letter will fit either. However, if you use envelopes when you mail out advertising to potential customers, use a No. 10. There is more room for materials to be inserted, and the increase in cost is very small.

Paper weight may be 16-lb., 20-lb., or 24-lb. basis weight, with the heavier stock being more expensive. Sixteen-pound is heavy enough, and sulphite bond is adequate and much cheaper than rag bond.

Envelopes are usually white, although they are available in many colors. Unless you are convinced that a colored envelope will earn more money it will probably be better to use white.

Envelopes are packed in boxes of 500. If you will use them to mail advertising, order at least 5000 at one time. If they will be used only for business correspondence, 1000 will last a long time.

Envelopes can be printed letterpress or offset, though letterpress may be less expensive since so little printing is needed on each piece. Assuming the printer has a type size and style you want, he can set up in a few minutes and be ready to print. If he does not, or if you want something unique and artistic for any reason, have an illustrator draw and letter your design oversize, at least four times final size. Take the artwork to your printer and order an *engraving* made, specifying the final size you want it to be. The result will be a block of wood with a zinc plate on one face, etched with your design. The printer puts it in his press and prints your envelopes.

If your printer sets the type for your envelope he will normally break up the form after printing, returning the type to the proper fonts. The next time you need envelopes (or any other printed matter which is reprinted periodically) you will have to pay again for typesetting, if your printing is done letterpress. Some printers will sell you the type as set and store it for you, thus eliminating additional typesetting charges. Eventually when you no longer need to use it for reprinting, the printer will often buy it back at the current scrap price for type metal. Ask your printer if he will provide you with this service.

Thermography is a variation of letterpress printing which produces raised lettering which can be felt with the fingertips and closely resembles expensive engraving. This process is often used on business cards, letterheads, and business envelopes. It is generally more expensive than normal flat printing by letterpress. Many of the firms who advertise business card printing also will print letterheads and envelopes by the thermograph process, but the choice of typefaces and sizes is somewhat limited.

LETTERHEAD

Your letterhead represents your company in the reader's hands. You will rarely write a personal business letter to a customer unless you operate a personal service business. Most of your letters will be to other businessmen, your suppliers. Your letterhead should be clean, attractive, and businesslike. It should not be "cute." Your printer can show you numerous sample letterheads and will gladly work with you in choosing a design and type which are right for your business.

The letterhead and envelope illustrated in figure 10-5 show the amount and kind of information normally included. It is not suggesting any particular style or type face since this must be your personal choice, guided by the type of product or service you sell.

Sixteen-pound white sulphite bond paper is recommended as an adequate compromise between quality and price. It is sturdy, lightweight, attractive, and low in cost. Two reams (a ream is 500 sheets) of printed letterheads will last a long time if used only for your business correspondence. You should order several thousand letterheads if they will be used for sales letters.

Letterpress is usually best and least expensive for printing letterheads and the same considerations apply as were discussed for envelopes. You should, however, have your printer print ten or more offset masters while he is printing your letterheads. (You can purchase these plasticized paper masters in office supply stores.) Put tissue inbetween the printed masters because the ink will stay wet, and carefully store them. When you next

Fig. 10–5 Letterhead and envelope.

need letterheads they can be rapidly printed offset from one of the paper masters, each of which is good for several thousand impressions. In this way you avoid paying again for typesetting and, since your paper masters have already been paid for, your subsequent letterheads will cost you only for paper and press time. This can represent a sizeable savings if you use many letterheads for sales letters or other direct mail advertising purposes.

BACK ORDER CARD

A back order card should be on hand for use when you suddenly get more orders than you have stock on hand to fill, or when shipments from your suppliers are late in arriving. These cards are not needed if you operate a service business only.

A typical back order announcement can be printed on a postcard. These can be ordinary postal cards or blank cards the same size if you do not want to tie up money in postage which may not be used for years. Blank cards are recommended.

Plain white cards can be used or you might consider light blue. The color is cool and restful which may be of help since you are telling the customer he will have to wait a bit before you can ship the order he has already paid for.

Of course, you should do your best to avoid back-ordering anything. It irritates your customer and can cost you some sales. At the very least it takes time, materials, and postage to notify your customers of the necessity for delay.

The wording of a typical back order card may be as follows:

AWFULLY SORRY FOR THE DELAY . . .

but orders have been arriving faster than our suppliers can cope with. We are temporarily out of stock but expect new supplies in a few days. Your very welcome order will be shipped to you in about _____ days or less.

Sincerely yours,
(facsimile signature)
Your name and title
Your company name and address

The headline should be in a large script typeface so that it looks friendly and sincere. Other, less formal wording for the headline might be "Oops! We goofed!" or "Oops! Sorry . . ."

The main thing is to let the customer know you are thinking about him. Let him know that you feel badly about the delay even if it isn't your fault (it certainly isn't his!), that you want to apologize, and assure him that his order will be shipped as soon as possible. If your apology has a bit of humor in it, which tends to put you down, it will be most effective. What you must make this card do for you is to calm your customer and make him willing to wait a bit and not cancel his order and ask for a refund. (Delayed shippings *can* mean trouble. They are discussed in chapter 11.)

If you have some inexpensive but useful novelty which you can offer your customer as a free gift to bear with you during your temporary difficulty, make the offer on the card. Be sure to note on each applicable file card in your order file that the free gift must be included when you finally do ship—and don't forget to do so!

SHIPPING LABEL

A shipping label will be necessary if you mail your own product or merchandise of any kind to your customers. It will also be required by most drop shippers who may mail your product for you. You can use stock labels, adding your company name and address with a rubber stamp, or you may have your labels printed. The latter is more costly but more businesslike.

The upper part of the label should contain your company name and address. The lower part should be blank so your customer's name and address can be typed in or so an address label can be pasted on.

Across the center of the label should appear one of the following legends, as appropriate:

MERCHANDISE: Open for inspection if necessary.
THIRD CLASS MAIL: Printed Matter.
BOOKS: SPECIAL FOURTH CLASS RATE.
POSTMASTER: If undeliverable, abandon.
PRINTED MATTER: Third or Fourth Class Rate paid as appropriate.

PURCHASE ORDER

If you deal in a product a purchase order may or may not be useful. Some companies will automatically extend normal 30-day credit to anyone who mails them a printed purchase order. Others will not extend credit unless your company has a good credit rating as attested to by a listing in *Dun & Bradstreet* or *Standard and Poor*. These reference volumes may be inspected at your public library or at your town's chamber of commerce.

Purchase orders will be useful in making local purchases of office supplies, printing, and other dealings with local businesses.

A purchase order is a legal instrument amounting to an offer to buy whatever is listed thereon at the agreed price. It is accepted in lieu of cash and becomes a collectable debt. Payment is normally expected within thirty days although many firms offer a small discount for payment made sooner. This may vary between $1/10$ of 1 percent to 3 percent or more for payment within ten days or slightly longer. Such discounts should always be taken if you have the cash on hand. They will add up to important money over a period of time. The cash discount for prompt payment offered to a user of a purchase order is not always available to the businessman who pays cash when making the same purchase! This is an additional reason for using purchase orders if they apply to your business.

An order can usually be placed by telephone, giving the seller the purchase order number, and later mailing your purchase order to the seller to confirm the telephoned order. This can save several days when you are in a hurry since your order can be processed and on the way to you before your purchase order arrives at the seller's place of business.

Each purchase order must be numbered. Your printer may be able to easily number each one in sequence, but if not, you can simply type in the number when you make out the purchase order. Start your numbering system with 1001—using numbers below 1000 screams out the fact that yours is a brand new business just getting started. So it may be, but in this case you shouldn't advertise the fact on paper.

The purchase order numbering system can be coded to indicate the calendar year by placing the last digit of the year before the actual number, separated from it by a dash. Thus, 9–1725 is a purchase order issued in 1979; 0–2447 is issued in 1980, etc. Or, if you wish, you can ignore the year coding and merely keep advancing one digit with each subsequent purchase order regardless of the year. This takes less time, and since it is also simple, straightforward and foolproof, it is recommended over other more complex methods.

Purchase orders require at least four copies. All except the original (first sheet) are printed on 9-lb. or 12-lb. tissue which is available in many colors: pink, blue, yellow, green, gold, white, and others. The first sheet is white, 16-lb. stock. The second sheet (tissue) should also be white. These two white copies are sent to the vendor (the seller). The two additional tissue copies should each be a different color: blue and pink, for example. The blue sheet should be placed in *numerical* order in a manila folder marked "Numerical File." The pink copy is filed alphabetically in another folder, the "Alphabetical File," by the vendor's company name. This enables you to check on orders either by the purchase order number or by the name of the vendor and will save considerable time searching your files. These two manila folders are kept in your file cabinet.

A suggested purchase order form is illustrated in figure 10-6. The various blanks in the sample purchase order have been given numbers which key them to the following numbered paragraphs. These numbers are not, of course, a part of the purchase order.

1. The number of the purchase order goes here.

2. Enter the date the purchase order is issued.

3. Enter the name and mailing address of the company to which the purchase order is being sent (the seller, supplier, or vendor).

4. Enter your company name and address, or the name and address of the company or person to whom you want the order shipped.

5. If you received a price quotation, put its number here. If your price came from a catalog or other source, note this here and explain in the body of the purchase order.

6. The time for delivery is given when you receive a quotation, and it also appears in many catalogs. You may also specify a period of time such as 30 days, 90 days, etc. Allow as much time as possible unless you must have the goods in a hurry. The time for delivery is usually stated as so many days ARO; *ARO* is a common abbreviation meaning "After Receipt of Order."

7. The vendor will often offer a discount for prompt payment when he

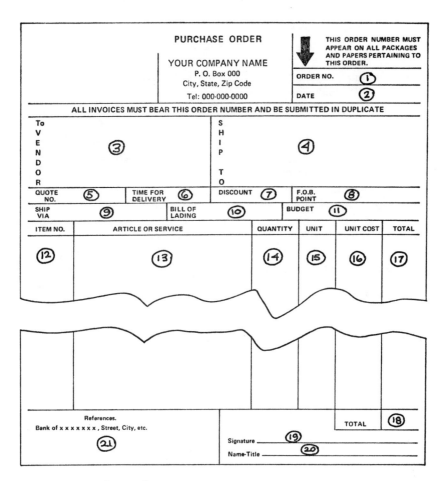

Fig. 10–6   Purchase order.

quotes a price to you. Enter the discount percentage and time period in this blank.

8. *FOB* means "Free on Board." In other words, the vendor places the shipment in the hands of the postal service, freight or express company, or shipping agent, but you pay the actual shipping costs on delivery from this point on. If the vendor pays shipping costs, enter the word "Destination" in this blank. If you must pay for shipping costs as a separate item, enter the words "Shipping Point" in this blank. Add a note to the purchase order specifying that the vendor prepay shipping costs and bill you for these costs on his invoice for the goods, showing shipping costs as a seperate item, if you prefer. You may also note on the purchase order to ship collect.

9. Normally you enter the words "Best Way" in this blank unless the

shipper has specified how he will ship or if you wish to specify a particular trucking line, air freight, bus, United Parcel Service, parcel post, or other means of transport.

10. The number of the bill of lading, if supplied by the vendor, is entered in this blank. Otherwise, leave it blank.

11. The budget blank is for entry of a code which identifies the expenditure according to one of the categories in your business expense files. You can devise your own code, using letters, numbers, or both. This is important in controlling expenditures and for your income tax records.

12. Each separate article or service included on the purchase order should receive an item number, starting with numeral 1.

13. Enter a *complete* description of the article or service you are ordering. Include catalog or stock number, color, size, and all other pertinent information to be sure of getting exactly what you desire.

14. Enter the quantity here for each numbered item on your purchase order—the amount of each you are ordering. For instance, if you are ordering 144 of something and the price is quoted by the dozen, you enter "12" here; and if the price is quoted by the gross, enter the figure "1."

15. The unit entered here is the same as the unit for which the price is quoted such as: gross, dozen, each, box, drum, roll, quart, bushel bundle, bag, ounce, pound, or other quantity.

16. Enter here the *price per unit.* (See 14 and 15 above.)

17. Enter the total price for each numbered item. This is the quantity (14) ordered, multiplied by the price per unit (16).

18. Enter here the sum total of all items in column 17. This figure is the total price for goods or services contracted for on the purchase order.

19. Your signature or the signature of an employee designated by you to sign purchase orders is signed in ink in this block.

20. The name and title of the person whose signature appears in blank 19 is typed in this space.

21. Financial references should be *printed* when your purchase orders are printed, or imprinted with your name and address if stock forms are used. As a minimum these references should include the name and address of your bank.

Having stock purchase order forms (ones you buy in an office supply store) imprinted to personalize them is the cheapest method of obtaining them. If you decide you must have your own design and want them at the lowest cost, have the copy set by photocomposition. Prepare a mechanical with this copy, using a lining pen (ruling pen) and India ink to draw in horizontal and vertical rules (lines). Have your purchase orders printed by offset. Letterpress can sometimes be used to advantage. However, the setting of vertical rules will add somewhat to the cost of composition since they are much more difficult to install than horizontal rules.

A quantity of 500 or 1000 units in white 16-lb. sulphite bond, and in 9-lb. or 12-lb. white, pink, and blue tissue, will last you a long time. You can save money by ordering these sheets printed loose and assembling them yourself when needed. The printer will, for an additional charge, assemble them into sets and pad them like a writing tablet. This is convenient and time-saving if your office is particularly busy, but otherwise it is an unnecessary expense. Purchase orders should be a standard 8½″ x 11″ size.

INVOICE

If you do not sell on credit you do not need invoices. Credit is not recommended for the vast majority of mail order operations, especially not for small companies just getting established.

A typical invoice is illustrated in figure 10-7. It must be submitted in duplicate which means you will need a minimum of four copies, the same as for purchase orders. Invoice blanks may be either 8½″ x 11″ or 5½″ x 8½″. They are prepared and numbered in the same manner as for purchase orders, and numerical and alphabetical files are maintained for

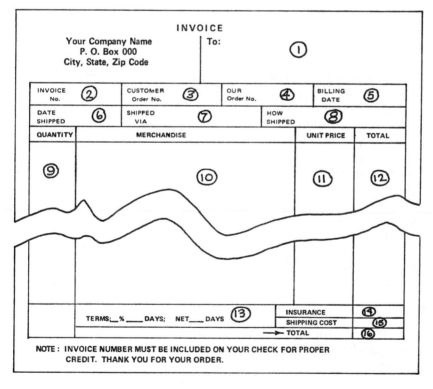

Fig. 10–7 Invoice.

invoices as described for purchase orders. Quantities of 1000 to 10,000 are typical for the usual credit business.

The numbers in the blanks on the sample invoice in figure 10-7 key them to the numbered paragraphs below.

1. Enter the name and address of the customer to whom the invoice is being sent.

2. Enter the number of the invoice according to whatever system you are using. Numbering systems described for purchase orders are applicable to invoices.

3. Enter the customer's purchase order number if applicable. Otherwise leave it blank or use any other applicable identification such as the date of his order.

4. Enter the number you have assigned to the customer's order. You will need a separate block of numbers for your credit shipments.

5. Enter the date the invoice is issued.

6. Enter the date the order was shipped to your customer.

7. Enter the shipping company or method of shipment.

8. Enter either "Prepaid" or "Collect," as appropriate.

9. Enter the quantity of each item shipped.

10. Enter the description of each item shipped.

11. Enter the price per unit.

12. Enter the total price for each item shipped.

13. Enter your terms here, namely, the amount of discount (if any) you are willing to allow for prompt payment. However, unless your sales are to other businesses rather than to individuals, do not offer a discount. Anything sold to individuals is normally billed as net (without discount). If no discount is offered, use the word "Net" and specify when you require payment: Net 30 days; Net 30 days EOM (means 30 days *after* the end of the month in which the invoice was mailed); Net 20 days; or other terms. A reasonably customary set of terms is 2% 10 days, net 30 days.

14. Enter the cost of insurance if it is to be paid by your customer.

15. Enter the shipping costs if you are prepaying the shipping costs (that is, if goods are shipped FOB Destination) but the customer is to reimburse you for them.

16. Enter the total cost of goods, insurance, and shipping charges, as applicable. This is the total the customer owes you and for which he is being billed.

REQUEST FOR QUOTATION

The request for quotation, usually abbreviated *RFQ*, will be needed if you use purchase orders and they can save you money even if you send cash with your orders. The RFQ is filled in, describing what you wish to purchase, and mailed to a number of possible suppliers. Each will then fill in the price at which he is willing to sell to you and his terms for payment.

When you receive the returned RFQs you will ordinarily place your order with the lowest bidder, assuming similar quality—the supplier who offers what you want at the lowest cost to you.

The prices you see in advertisements and catalogs are *not* always firm. An RFQ will often secure a better price, especially if you are purchasing a quantity of an item for resale. There are quantity discounts as well as prompt payment discounts available on practically every imaginable product.

A minimum of five copies of an RFQ are required although, unlike purchase orders, all can be of the same color. Four copies are mailed to each possible supplier; two will be returned. The remaining copy is held in a numerical RFQ file.

When two copies of the RFQ are returned from each supplier, inspect them for price, discounts offered, shipping costs, delivery schedules, and any substitutions suggested by the supplier. Select the lowest cost source of *acceptable* merchandise and place an order with him. One copy from the successful supplier is filed in an alphabetical RFQ file folder. The other of his copies replaces the existing copy in the numerical file. The remaining RFQs are held in a separate folder until the ordered merchandise is received from the successful bidder, as insurance against his being unable for any reason (fire, strikes, or other) to fill your order. In this event, you still have RFQs from other bidders and can place an order with one of them. When merchandise is received and found satisfactory, all RFQs *except* one numerical and one alphabetical file copy from the successful bidder are destroyed. Don't clutter up your limited file space with unneeded papers. Necessary papers will accumulate rapidly enough.

In determining which quotation is actually low, you must consider not only the quoted price but also the prompt payment discount when offered. An offer of $98.25 net is higher in cost than $100 with 2%–10 day terms, which actually costs you $100 less 2 percent, or $98 net if paid within ten days of receipt of the seller's invoice. True, the savings is only a quarter, but at least it pays for nearly all the postage for the RFQ and purchase order. Always take full advantage of any cash discount offered if you have the necessary cash on hand. These small discounts will add up rapidly and become sizeable savings for you. Taking advantage of discounts is good business practice.

Figure 10-8 illustrates a request for quotation suitable for mail order businesses. It should be 8½″ x 11″ in size and can be printed on white paper. Colored stock is not necessary nor desirable for your RFQ. The numbers in the blanks of the sample RFQ are keyed to the paragraphs below. (The unnumbered blanks on the RFQ will be filled in by the person making the quote. These are self-explanatory.)

1. Enter the number of the RFQ.
2. Enter the date the RFQ is made out.

3. Enter the latest date for goods or services to be received by you.

4. Place an "X" in the FOB Destination box. The quoter will change this if he will not quote FOB Destination. In this case he will note the FOB point, usually his factory or warehouse.

5. Insert the date you wish all quotes to be in your hands. You should allow at least two weeks and preferably longer.

6. Enter the name and address of the supplier to whom the RFQ is sent.

7. Number each item for which a quote is desired.

8. Enter the description, stock number, or other complete description of each item to be quoted.

9. Enter the quantity or amount of each item.

10. Enter the appropriate unit: dozen, gross, case, box, etc.

REFUND SLIP

There are always a few customers who request a refund of their money, but never very many. Some will be truthfully dissatisfied, probably

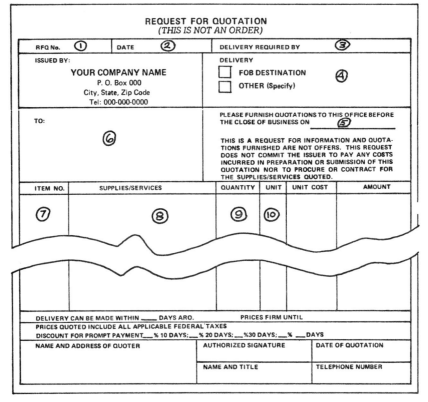

Fig. 10–8 Request for quotation.

because they did not really know what they were buying. A few will be dishonest in that they have used your product until they no longer needed it and then will return it for refund. It is sometimes difficult to separate legitimate refund requests from the cheaters. It will be best if you honor all requests for refund which are accompanied by the returned merchandise, even if it cannot be resold. Various methods of eliminating refund requests were discussed in earlier chapters and if the advice given there is heeded you will have very few refunds to make.

Refund requests should be processed as they arrive, at least no later than the following business day. Make out the check and rubber-stamp it "Refund Check." Insert the check and one refund slip in an envelope and mail it to the customer.

Refund slips should be printed on 3¼″ x 6″ pieces of lightweight paper. These slips will fit into a No. 6 (small size) envelope. The slip should be clipped or stapled to the check. Wording on a typical refund slip may be as follows:

> The refund you have requested is enclosed. We are sorry that you were not completely satisfied but are pleased to fulfill our celebrated Guarantee of Satisfaction or your money back.
>
> We value our customers highly and consider them our friends. We hate to lose a friend, and would like to notify you when we discover something else which may interest you.
>
> Sincerely yours,
(facsimile signature)
Your name and title
Your company name and address

CHECK REQUEST

You will receive a large number of personal checks drawn on out-of-state banks. A very few of them will, for one reason or another, not be honored when presented for collection. Rarely is the issuer of a bad check knowingly dishonest; besides, knowingly sending a bad check through the mail is a federal offense. Usually the sender thinks he has a larger balance than he actually has in his account, or he may withdraw money before the check reaches his bank, leaving insufficient funds.

There are several approaches to this problem. One is to assume all checks are good and ship orders as received. Bad checks are retained and show up in your records as a business loss deductible from income before taxes. This is best if your product is a high-profit item, and especially if it sells to the customer for $10 or less.

A check returned for any reason *except* "No Such Account" or "Account Closed" should be redeposited after thirty days. Many of them will go through and be honored the second time.

It is possible to eliminate bad check losses by shipping the order only after the check clears. However, this can take as long as six weeks, and such a delay is unacceptable to most customers (see the section on shipping delays in chapter 11). If you delay shipping until a check clears, you are likely to get more order cancellations and refund requests than your potential losses from bad checks. Likewise, insistence on a money order and refusal to even accept personal checks will drastically cut the number of orders you receive, simply because it is far less convenient for your customer to buy a money order than it is to write a personal check. You *must* make it as easy as possible for your customers to order from you.

If a short shipping delay (one week or ten days) is acceptable, you can, for a slight additional cost, collect each check before shipping. Send out a letter worded similarly to this:

Date:
To: Customer's Bank
The enclosed check is drawn against Account No.   in the amount of $ payable to the undersigned.
Please honor the enclosed check and issue a bank check to our order. A stamped, self-addressed envelope is enclosed for your convenience.
Thank you.

Sincerely yours,
(facsimile signature)
Your name and title
Your company name and address

Mail it to the bank on which the check is drawn, enclosing a stamped, self-addressed envelope. If the check is valid, the bank will accept it and issue you a bank check for the full amount less charges for the check, if any. Check charges are usually 10¢ to 25¢. Total postage will be 30¢ (1979). Cost of envelopes and check request form will add another 3¢ or 4¢ to this total. Your profit margin must be sufficiently large to absorb approximately 60¢ on each order if this method is used, and still give you the profit you need.

However, because of the additional cost and work and the fact that the vast majority of checks you receive will be collectible, your annual net profits will probably be larger if you ship all orders as received and absorb any bad checks as business losses.

BAD CHECK NOTICE

If you absorb bad checks as a business expense you may still be willing to spend 15¢ on each in an attempt to collect. If a check does not clear after the second time it is deposited, a form like this one may be filled in and mailed to the customer involved:

Dear
    Your check No.   in the amount of $ has been returned not paid by
    We realize this oversight is accidental on your part so we have shipped your order on
    Since we cannot resubmit your original check for collection, would you please send us a money order, cashier's check or certified check for $ due us for your order?
    Thank you.

                  Sincerely yours,
                  (facsimile signature)
                  Your name and title
                  Your company name and address

A self-addressed (but not stamped or postage paid) envelope may be enclosed to make it easier for the customer to pay his debt to you. If you receive no reply, consider the bad check a loss and note this information on the customer's card in the completed section of your order file. However, most customers will pay you when notified in a nice way that their check bounced.

11

When Money and Orders Arrive

A few days after magazines carrying your first classified ads are mailed to subscribers and appear on the newsstands, your mail will bring inquiries. You must be prepared to answer these within 24 hours. Some of the inquiries you answer will result in orders starting to come in within a week or two.

Before inquiries arrive, you must have stock available to fill expected orders and arrangements made to replenish your stock as needed. All your direct mail advertising materials must be printed and on hand, ready to mail to prospective customers as inquiries come in. Your office must be equipped and set up. Files must be ready. You must have postage stamps on hand. In other words, your business operation must be organized and ready to function smoothly and efficiently when it is "switched on" by the arrival of the first batch of inquiries.

If you deal in a product, you will have located one or more sources of supply through mailing out your requests for quotations. You will have ordered an initial quantity for delivery before your first ads reach the public. If you deal in a service, you will have made all the necessary arrangements and contacts ahead of time.

All your initial printing of business forms and advertising materials will have been completed. You will have obtained your business reply permit from the U.S. Postal Service (in case you use this method) early enough that your printer can place your permit number on your envelopes.

Your office and work space will have been established and equipped, and files and shelves for printed matter and stock prepared and installed.

Your classified ads will have been prepared and placed, and the periodicals selected in which they will appear in the future. The ads will have been placed well before deadlines so that you know exactly when the

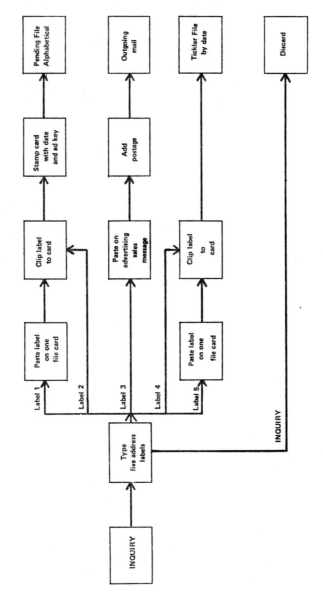

Fig. 11–1 Inquiry handling: operational flow diagram.

public will first see them. You will also have ordered publication of your ads in subsequent issues so there will be no months when your ad does not appear in some periodical.

Very probably you will have everything ready before your ads appear. This slack time gives you a breathing space which, as your business grows, you may never have again. Use it for a brief vacation if you wish. Or use it to stuff envelopes or self-mailers with advertising materials. The more of these you have ready ahead of time for mailing, the more rapidly you can respond to inquiries. Since you will very shortly be receiving orders and money as well as inquiries in the same mail delivery, prestuffed mailings will simplify your operation.

HANDLING INQUIRIES

Figure 11-1 shows a flow diagram to guide you in handling inquiries. Refer to this chart as you read through the procedures below.

Potential customers will reply to your classified ad by either postcard or letter. *Always* staple the envelope to the letter since not everyone will include his name and address in a letter. Separate cards and letters into two stacks. Carefully inspect each one to be sure you can decipher names address, and zip code. Set aside those without complete addresses or which are unreadable.

Interleave four sheets of carbon paper or carbon film with five sheets of gummed, perforated, address labels and place it in your typewriter. Type each name and address on a label. This produces an original and four carbon copies. Paste one label on each of two 3″ x 5″ file cards. Clip one label to each of these cards. Place one card in your Tickler File under today's date. Stamp the remaining card with the date and the ad key and place it in alphabetical order in your Pending File. Paste the remaining label on the folder or envelope containing your advertising sales message, order blank, and return envelope (also marked with the ad key.) This you will mail to the potential customer.

The original inquiry may now be discarded since you have no further use for it.

HANDLING ORDERS

An order-handling operations flow diagram is illustrated in figure 11-2. Refer to this diagram for the following discussion.

Orders will arrive in envelopes, usually in the reply envelope you provided. Separate these reply envelopes from the remainder of your mail, most of which will consist of inquiries. Inquiries should be handled *after* processing all orders as described below.

Open the reply envelopes, setting aside those which do not contain payment. Those containing some form of payment should have envelope, order blank, and payment (check, money order, or cash) fastened together with a paper clip. Place these in a separate stack.

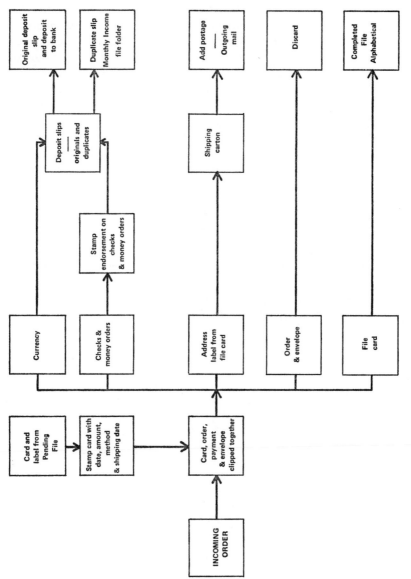

Fig. 11-2   Order handling: operational flow diagram.

Remove the file cards from your Pending File for each of the orders you received. Note on each card the date the order was received, the amount paid, the method of payment, and the date the order will be shipped. Temporarily clip this card to the order.

When all orders have been treated as described, separate cash into one pile, and checks and money orders into another. Stamp your endorsement on the back of each check and money order. Make up a deposit slip in duplicate, entering each check, money order, and the total amount of cash separately. Place the deposit with the original deposit slip in an envelope ready to be taken to the bank. File the duplicate deposit slip on the order spike or in the current month's file folder as described in chapter 10.

Prepare your product for shipment. Normally you will have already packed these in shipping cartons and affixed blank shipping labels. Detach the extra address label from the file card and place it in the proper location on the shipping carton. Affix the proper postage on the carton and place it in your outgoing mail.

At this time place the file card alphabetically in your Completed File. Discard the order blank or letter and its envelope since these are of no further value.

Occasionally you will receive an order which contains no payment. Usually this results from an honest error although there are always a few persons who will consistently try to get something for nothing. Treat all such orders as legitimate since most will be.

Below is a typically worded message which you can have printed on a card to mail to the customer to inform him that his order did not include payment.

> Thank you for your order for ___(PRODUCT OR SERVICE)___ which we received on ___ 19 . Unfortunately, your payment was not enclosed with your order. Since we wish to save you the additional cost of C.O.D. shipment, we will hold your order until we receive your payment of ___ due on this order. May we anticipate hearing from you very soon?
>
> Your company name and address

Fill in the blanks on the notice form, address it to the customer, add the correct amount of postage for a postcard, and place it in your outgoing mail. At the same time, place his order in a manila folder marked "Hold for Payment" and place the folder in your file cabinet.

USING THE TICKLER FILE

Figure 11-3 shows a flow diagram illustrating the use of the Tickler File in the daily operation of your business. Refer to this illustration for the following discussion.

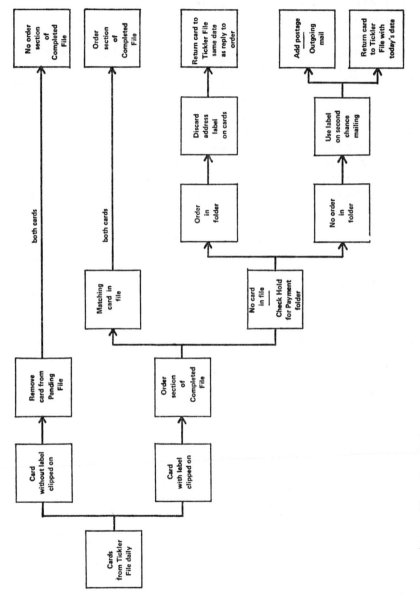

Fig. 11–3   Tickler File: operational flow diagram.

The Tickler File is a temporary file which helps considerably in smoothing the operation of your business and enables you to keep current in all its phases. You should check this file every day, although if you wish you can check the weekend dates on the following Monday. *Do not skip this daily chore. It is very important.*

The Tickler File contains addressed file cards with an extra address label clipped to each of them, filed numerically by days of the month. Each day the cards for that day's date should be removed from the file. They have been in the file for 30 or 60 days and some action will be required, as explained below.

With these cards in hand, check first the Order section of the Completed File. If the matching card is there, indicating an order has been received and processed, file the two cards together in the Completed File. Discard the address label.

If there is no matching card there, check the Hold for Payment folder. If a matching order is in this folder, note the date it was received and refile the card in the Tickler File for that day of the month. Discard the address label.

If no matching order card or order is present, this informs you that it is time to offer the potential customer a second chance to order. Remove the clipped-on address label from the card and set it aside. Replace the card in the Tickler File into today's date section. The address label will be used to mail a follow-up sales message to the potential customer.

If any of these cards removed from the Tickler File *do not* have an extra address label clipped to them, this means that it has been 60 days since the first inquiry and also that you have mailed a second-chance offer 30 days ago. For all practical purposes the name on the card no longer represents a prospective customer but it still has some value. Remove the matching card from the Pending File and place both cards in the No Order section of the Completed File.

SECOND CHANCE MAILINGS
AND SPECIAL OFFERS

Your second chance offer should be ready to mail to those who inquired but did not place an order within 30 days. It is the last opportunity you have to gain these persons as customers. You must do your best to make a sale with this mailing. It must have a strong appeal for the hesitant customer.

There are numerous ways to present your message effectively, as described in chapters 7 and 9. You will need at least one new mailing piece which the customer has not seen. This can be combined with one or more other sales appeals. Your mailing must also include another order blank and reply envelope to make ordering as easy as possible.

A typical, effective second chance mailing might consist of the following items, all enclosed in an envelope for mailing:

Sales letter
Same mailing piece as previously used
Order blank
Reply envelope
Special offers, reduced price, free bonus, etc.
Any novelty you feel might help make the sale

SPECIAL OFFERS

It is legitimate to offer an additional useful but low-cost item as an added inducement to buy. This might consist of whatever you originally offered as a free bonus for quick ordering, making the offer anew, or something entirely different. This often will cause the hesitant customer to make up his mind and order from you.

Another method of inducement is a reduced price. This works part of the time but makes customers wonder why it was first offered to him at a higher price. You will have to convince him that your reduced price offer is not a usual thing but that there is a legitimate reason why you can make such an offer *at this time*. Some possible reasons might include:

Reducing inventory prior to moving to new quarters
Reducing inventory to reduce tax liabilities in states imposing an inventory tax
Selling out existing stock because of model change (New color, shape, style, etc.)
Reducing stock to ease inventory taking
Making room for new shipments arriving soon
End of month (or year) clearance sale

If you use one of the above or a similar reason to justify a special reduced price to the customer, be certain you can justify it as truthful in case the Federal Trade Commission asks. They probably won't and reduced prices are a customary way of inducing sales, but laws are on the books forbidding preferential treatment of customers.

It is easy to "move" from one room to another. Inventory tax reasons are legitimate. New stock may appear slightly different or can be so ordered. It is always legitimate to try to sell as much stock as possible before taking inventory. If you have an order for stock which is outstanding you may legitimately need room for it. The clearance sale is borderline and theoretically *all* customers should receive the new low price at this time.

Second Chance Sales Letter

A sales letter is one of the more effective ways of increasing sales in a second chance mailing. It should be printed on your letterhead or a facsimile thereof, on 12-lb or 16-lb paper, but it is not economical to put much added expense into this sales letter reproduction. Only a small percentage of those who receive this second chance mailing will send you an order. Therefore the costs of this mailing should be kept as low as possible. It must be paid for out of the profits gleaned from second chance orders, and not charged off against orders resulting from your initial mailings.

In many towns and cities there are small shops which advertise "Printing While You Wait," offering to print 100 copies of 8½" x 11" from your original copy (prepared mechanical or typed material) for a few dollars, or a few cents a copy. Larger quantities will be printed more cheaply. This can be a bargain for much of your sales material and you should investigate such a shop if one is located in your vicinity. Usually these shops are equipped with an ITEK photographic plate-making camera and a number of offset presses. If your original copy is in good, clean condition, the results will be most satisfactory.

If you secured several paper offset masters imprinted with your letterhead when it was printed, you can prepare the plate for the sales letter yourself at a very low cost. You will need to purchase (1) a typewriter ribbon designed especially for preparing offset masters, (2) a special nonreproducible pencil with brown lead, and (3) a special reproducible pencil with black lead. An office supply or graphic arts store should stock these items. Both pencils and typewriter ribbon will be plainly marked with their intended use. Addressograph-Multigraph nonreproducible pencils are painted brown while their reproducible pencils are painted red. Other brands are available.

Be extremely careful in handling paper masters, holding them only by the edges, and be sure your hands are clean and dry. Fingerprints, even if you can't see them, are oily and will take ink on the press, making the master unusable. Use a ruler or T-square and the nonreproducible pencil to block out the page size and typing area with lightly drawn lines on the surface of the master. If the spool of the special ribbon does not fit your typewriter, rewind the ribbon on an empty spool which does fit.

Insert the paper master in your typewriter, align it, and type your sales message as if it were a normal letter. Go slowly and try not to make an error. Errors can be erased if done extremely carefully and lightly with a nonabrasive eraser such as Pink Pearl. Try to disturb the surface of the master as little as possible. It is not necessary to completely remove the error. A ghost image which is very light will not print. If the erasure goes through the prepared surface to expose the paper backing, the master will print a blot of ink at this point, making it unusable. When done typing the offset master, store the ribbon in foil or plastic to keep it moist for future use.

When you prepare your letter for printing, leave space for the date and the addressee's name and address if you wish to personalize your letters. Otherwise, no date is needed and your letter can open with a simple salutation. This should be asexual: a phrase like "Dear Customer" is preferred.

The text of a typical second chance sales letter is given in figure 11-4. The name of the product is mentioned 3 times. The pronoun *you* or *yours* is used 34 times. The letter is written in a personal vein and signed by the president of the company (you can sign your name on a paper master, using the reproducible pencil). A bonus is offered for quick responses. Action is stressed in that an order is asked for "within 10 days" and "right away," both in the final paragraph.

Normally you should be able to say all that is necessary in a sales letter on one side of the page. Few persons will bother to read beyond this, although you can use the back of the letter for additional copy if you wish. This requires a second master and a second press run, both of which add to your costs. Approach the copy of your sales letter with the same ideas in mind that have been stressed for writing your follow-up mailing pieces.

HANDLING LETTERS FROM CUSTOMERS

Before you have been in business very long you will begin to receive letters from your customers which are neither inquiries nor orders. Practically all of these will be from persons who have purchased your product or service and they will have something to say about it.

The most valuable of these letters are those which praise your product or service, the unsolicited testimonial, and those which suggest new products or services or which contain useful hints and suggestions adaptable to your business. There will also be letters from customers who are less than satisfied. These can be equally valuable if they contain valid complaints.

All customer letters *should* be answered courteously and as soon as possible. They *must* be answered if your product or service is such that you can reasonably expect prompt orders from your customers. Unanswered letters cause customers to become irritated, and they usually then speak disparagingly of your company to their friends.

In most mail order businesses such bad word-of-mouth advertising will not adversely affect your sales volume or profits. Customers are scattered throughout the 50 states and probably some foreign countries. For the same reason, good word-of-mouth advertising will seldom be of much value to a mail order company, although it will always bring more inquiries and some new orders.

COMPANY LETTERHEAD

Dear Customer:

A month ago I mailed you at your request complete
details describing what the valuable new book, MAIL
ORDER: STARTING UP, MAKING IT PAY, can do for you.
Since your order has not as yet been received, I won-
dered if perhaps you had some doubt of your personal
chances for success in mail order.

I'd like to put your mind at ease. If you follow
the clearly presented instructions in MAIL ORDER:
STARTING UP, MAKING IT PAY you are assured of receiving
numerous inquiries and orders and can anticipate a
successful, growing business. Your income can be as
large as you need. You don't have to wait for years
and never again will you have to ask for a raise! You,
and only you, control the size of your income.

There is room for many thousands more mail order
companies. Yours can be one of them. By answering our
ad you proved you have the desire to be your own boss,
to control and increase your income, to have the luxuries
a larger income will bring to you and your family. But
you must act now. Every day you delay starting your own
successful easy-money business you are losing money.

To help you get started I am extending our offer
of a complete set of printed forms needed in your
business, which will be included absolutely free with
your copy of MAIL ORDER: STARTING UP, MAKING IT PAY if
you will send your order with 10 days from the date
stamped on the enclosed order blank. A postage paid
envelope is included for your convenience in ordering.
May we expect your order right away?

                              Sincerely yours,
                              (facsimile signature)
                              John A. Smith
                              President

Fig. 11–4 Second chance sales letter.

Whether you answer all, some, or none of your customers' letters is a personal decision you will have to make. Answering letters takes time and costs money. While it builds good will, it may not increase your profits enough to cover its cost.

Each incoming letter should be opened and the envelope stapled to the letter. Read each letter, making notes in the margins or the envelope, commenting on the contents. This is a good idea whether you intend to answer it or not.

Check these incoming letters against those in your correspondence file. In case the same person has written before, previous correspondence may be in the file and should be inspected while the new letter is being considered.

As the letters are read, separate them into three piles. In one, place all the letters which tell of satisfaction with your product or service. In another, place all letters which suggest improvements or changes in your operation, pro and con. In the third and very smallest pile, put the crank letters. You'll rarely receive any of these but you may occasionally receive insulting mail which appears to have been written by someone crazed. All letters you wish to keep should be filed in your correspondence file along with carbon copies of your replies, if any.

TESTIMONIAL LETTERS

Letters expressing satisfaction and happiness with your product or service are often received. Some of these may sound so exaggerated that they seem humorous. However, many of them can be excerpted and quoted in your sales literature. Such testimonials are potent sales helps.

Before you can legally use an *entire* letter, or quote from it and *name* the writer, you *must* obtain his written permission. Under the law, the contents of a letter remain the property of the writer and may not be revealed except at the risk of being guilty of invasion of privacy. You could also be successfully sued for civil damages. So do not use the writer's name in your advertising unless you have obtained written permission from the sender of each letter. You can, however, print excerpts blind: that is, with the initials of the writer and his state.

Reply to testimonial letters first, thanking the writer. Those letters which are so worded that they would be valuable testimonials to the worth *to the customer* of your product or service are the ones you may wish to ask permission to use in your advertising. If the customer suggests being paid for his permission, thank him in a nice way but decline to accept such an arrangement. Paid testimonials are worth absolutely nothing in your advertising. Only unsolicited testimonials freely given to you have value, and they should be identified as unsolicited in your advertising.

In your advertising, introduce the testimonials with a statement worded similarly to the following:

> These unsolicited testimonials from a few of our many satisfied customers tell you, in their own words, what they feel about (PRODUCT OR SERVICE). The original letters from which these excerpts were taken are on file in our main offices and may be inspected upon request during normal business hours.

Naturally, you will not be visited by prospective customers wishing to examine your files. However, you *may* have a visit from representatives of the U.S. Postal Service or Federal Trade Commission. Their interest will be only in assuring that you actually have in your files the testimonial letters claimed in your advertising, to protect customers against fraud. Just be sure you have the actual letters, maintained in a separate file folder with any required permission to quote, before you make any statements in print regarding testimonials from satisfied customers.

By the way, these are the *only* files subject to such inspection. All other files and records are confidential unless voluntarily opened by you or subpoenaed by a court of law.

LETTERS WITH SUGGESTIONS

Reply to all letters containing suggestions, thanking the writer courteously for his trouble in writing to you. Do not discuss the suggestion in any way. Do not say you intend to take the writer's advice or that you will adopt his suggestion. Be very noncommittal in your reply but don't be obviously vague. Merely expressing your thanks and commenting that the writer's remarks are interesting is sufficient. Do not write in such a manner which could cause the writer to reply and attempt to start up a correspondence. If this happens, a formal note of thanks, *printed, not typed,* on a postcard will usually halt the flood of letters from this source.

CRANK LETTERS

There are only two ways to handle crank letters. Either answer them with a printed form letter or card expressing thanks or good wishes, or ignore them. Ignoring them is cheaper.

However, letters containing threats or which are obscene in content can be given to your local postmaster for transmittal to the postal inspector in the writer's home area. Such letters should never be answered. Both letters and envelopes should be taken to your postmaster.

FORMAL REPLY CARD

Cards should be printed with a formal thank-you note for use in acknowledging letters which do not require nor merit a personal reply. A text similar to the following is recommended:

Dear Customer:

Thank you for your recent communication. We appreciate very much your taking the time to write to us.

Please accept our thanks and our every good wish for your continued health and happiness.

Sincerely yours,

(FACSIMILE SIGNATURE)

Your name and title

Your company name and address

SHIPPING DELAYS

Your customer has the right to know when his order will be shipped to him. If you promise to "rush" his order, this means right away—a few days, not to exceed a week. However, if you do not make such a promise and do not state when you will ship, you must ship the order within 30 days. If you do *not* ship when you say you will, or within 30 days if no specific promise is made, you must notify the customer and give him the option of (1) canceling his order and getting an immediate refund of all the money he paid you, or (2) agreeing to wait until another specified shipping date. You must also provide your customer with a prepaid postcard so he can state his decision to you at no cost to him. *This is very important!*

If your later specified shipping date represents a delay of 30 days or less, *no reply* from your customer can be considered an agreement to the new shipping date. If the later shipping date represents a delay beyond 30 days, your customer *must* give his consent to the delay. If he does not do so, you *must* return *all* your customer's money at the end of the first 30 days of delay.

If you or your customer cancel the order, you must return *all* the money he sent you in full within seven days after the order is cancelled. If you are selling on credit, you can take as long as one full billing cycle to make this adjustment. If, however, you deal in certain services you are not legally bound by the seven-day rule. These include such services as photo finishing; magazine or newsletter subscriptions which are delivered serially; C.O.D. orders; orders on credit where billing is not made until shipment is made; and sales similar to book club sales where the customer must inform you before the shipping date that he does not wish the merchandise.

In any case, it will pay you to bend over backwards in treating your customers fairly, especially in making refunds, or you may miss out on future orders he may place with you. Honesty pays, especially in mail order!

Most mail order operators place great reliance on repeat orders to maintain and expand their businesses. Contented customers can be one of your greatest assets. It is only good business to deal fairly, provide fast shipment and good value, and please your customers so they will send you additional orders, and will tell their friends about you.

12 Increasing Your Business and Income

There are a number of choices open to you which will increase your sales and therefore your income. Depending upon the particular type of business you have, you can consider adding additional products or services or both. These should be of a sort which will tie in with your operation and be of interest to the customers whose names are in your Completed File as well as those who read your ads.

TIE-IN PRODUCTS AND SERVICES

A tie-in product is one which can be used in the same field in which your main product is intended for use.

Tie-in products and services can be offered in separate classified ads, and they can also be offered directly to those who inquire about or order another of your products. A combination of these two methods will usually provide the greatest increase in income for you. No matter what product you use to establish your business, there will be numerous other products which you can use as tie-ins to broaden your scope of operation.

Below are listed some typical products and services with possibilities for tie-ins. Of course, any listed tie-in product could be a main product, and vice versa.

Hunting Knife—Sharpening stone, match safe, compass, signal mirror, leather waterproofing, belts, holsters, first aid kits, snakebite kit, haversack, tarpaulin, sleeping bag, books on hunting, fishing, boating, camping, bicycling, backpacking.

Auto wax kit—Nameplate, monogram initials, vanity mirror, first aid kit, kit of "forgettable" items, tire pressure gauge, snow and ice scraper, sponge and squeegee, toys and games for children riding in cars, windshield defogger, car crib, car play pen.

Travelbooks—Maps, currency converter, map route marking service for vacations, language phrase books, language tapes and records.

How-to-do-it books—Construction plans, blueprints, special tools, bargain tools, craft materials, locator service for plans and materials.

Personal printed stationery—Personalized memo pads, business cards, fun motto cards, ballpoint pens, address labels, imprinted pencils and pens, typewriter ribbons, typing service, calendars, engagment and appointment books, diaries, iron-on patterns for T-shirts.

Fishing lures—Tackle of all sorts, fishing calendar, books on fishing, fish bait, recipes, fish location maps, fishing thermometer, how to raise worms and crickets for bait.

Remail service—Mail forwarding, confidential address and/or telephone service, sales of picture postcards and folders.

Research service—Purchasing service for books, manuscript typing and advice service, sales of market lists and marketing tips for beginning writers, editing and rewrite, ghost writing, literary criticism.

Reminder service—Sale of greeting cards, flower and gift order service, gift buying and mailing service.

The above are only a few of many possibilities and are included to indicate the many different products and services which are suitable for tie-in sales. A combination of products and services which logically belong together is a solid foundation for successful expansion.

ADVERTISING YOUR TIE-INS

The time to consider tie-ins is when your business is young and just starting to grow. Although results will be slower in coming it will be less expensive at this stage to offer your tie-ins directly to those who inquire about your advertised product or service and to those who eventually order from you. This can be handled by direct mail advertising. You should prepare sales messages, offers, order blanks, etc. for your tie-ins and include these in the mailing you make when inquiries start to arrive.

This method of advertising your tie-ins has several advantages. Those who reply to your classified ads are already interested in at least one item you advertised. When they receive your mailing they not only receive the information they asked for but are also confronted with one or more offers of additional similar items. The person who is interested in buying a knife, for instance, is also likely to be interested in buying a sharpening stone, and very possibly in other related items. Thus, many orders you receive for the specific item mentioned in your classified ad will also include orders for your tie-ins. Too, some of those who do not decide to purchase your advertised item will send in orders for tie-ins. These extra orders greatly increase your income and cost you almost nothing to secure. They also make customers out of far more inquirers than would happen without tie-in offers.

It will also be advantageous to include tie-in sales messages with each order you ship. The cost is minimal and some of these will result in additional orders. The customer may have lost or discarded the information you previously sent. He may currently decide he wants something else you are offering. He may suddenly have more money to spend than he had earlier. He may be influenced by the quality of what he has purchased when he has it in his hand and thus be inclined to order additional items from you. There are many unknown reasons the customer may be more willing to buy at one time than another. What you must do is make it as easy as possible for him to buy, and to remind him occasionally of all the things you have to offer.

As your business expands and you include more tie-ins in your product line, mail these *new* offers periodically to your old customers and inquirers whose cards are in your Completed File. Mailings should be made at approximately three- to six-month intervals and each should offer at least two or three *new* items. You can also enclose sales materials on existing items since the customer may now be in the market for them although he was not the last time you contacted him. The new items you offer serve as a welcome introduction for the materials he has seen before. Each of these mailings will result in more orders, bringing in additional profits and further increasing your income.

Eventually you will want to further increase your orders, and to do this you must get more potential customers to respond to your ads. This means you will have to write new ads describing one or more of your *new* items. Your old ads will still be running, of course, but now you will have two or more *different* classified ads appearing in some or all of the periodicals you are using, under the same or different classifications. This ensures that more people will see and respond to your ads. To use the simple "knife—sharpening stone" example, if *both* are advertised you will get knife orders from sharpening stone owners and orders for sharpening stones from those who already own knives.

The new classified ads for additional items should be keyed to identify the publication. You should also key these ads to identify *the particular ad* which prompted each inquiry. The results show pulling power for ads for different items and can serve as a guide to the type of items your readers are interested in. This information assists you in choosing additional items to add to your product line. You will also use this information to determine when it is time to drop an item from your line, having a close-out sale if you have money in stock when interest begins to lag.

It will rarely pay to run separate classified ads for *each* item in your line. Use classified ads only for those which seem to have the greatest reader interest and which have high profit margins. Advertise your biggest sellers in your classified ads. Let your direct mail sales messages sell the rest.

When considering whether to devote a separate classified ad to a new item, decide whether it would pay its way if it was your only source of income. If it will, you should probably advertise it separately. If it won't, it should not be separately advertised since it is incapable of paying its own way and producing enough income to give you a suitable profit. However, due to the low cost of your mailing piece inserts it can be introduced to your customers in this way and will bring in additional income.

CONTROL OF TIE-IN ADVERTISING

Tie-in sales messages included as part of your normal reply to inquiries are automatically controlled through operation of the filing system described in chapter 11. No additional control is needed, although you might wish to keep track of inquiries prompted by *new* classified ads if these have been keyed by product as well as periodical. This is accomplished by use of additional charts as illustrated in figures 10-1 and 10-3, one for each product featured in a classified ad.

When you make a direct mailing of new item offers to names in your Completed File, remove both cards and treat them exactly as if they were new inquiries as described in chapter 11, adding the new date and noting what is being mailed. Temporarily file them in the Pending and Tickler files after the address labels are prepared and the mailing made. (Put the date-stamped card in your Pending File and the unstamped card in the Tickler File. All orders will thus be noted on the same card while the other remains blank.) Control from this point is automatic through the normal operation of your filing system. Both cards will eventually end up in the Completed File as they did before.

When removing these cards initially from the Completed File, note whether they were taken from the order or no order sections. If taken from the Order section, make out a duplicate card on a *colored* card and temporarily place this in the No Order section. Should no order be received from this mailing, both cards would normally end up in the No Order section; however, the existence of the colored duplicate card found here will remind you to place both cards in the Order section since one order or more has already been received from this particular customer. Thus, all the cards in the Order section remain valid names for your mailing list of mail order buyers.

LEASING YOUR MAILING LISTS

As your business grows you will gradually accumulate a large number of cards in both the Order and No Order sections of your Completed File. These cards represent a valuable commodity. All show names of persons who have replied to a classified ad placed by a mail order company. Those who actually ordered from you are those who have actually *bought* from a mail order company. As such, they become the nucleus of mailing lists which can serve as an additional source of income for you.

When these files are nearly full, take one section at a time and set up two additional card files. These new files are called "Mailing List—Purchasers" and "Mailing List—Inquirers." Use 52 dividers in each file. Mark the dividers with the names of the 50 states, the District of Columbia, and Foreign.

Within the inquirers file, place one set of cards from the No Order section of your Completed File. File these by zip code (this is essential for leasing your list). Do the same in the purchasers file with duplicate cards from the Order section of your Completed File.

Mailing lists are compiled and marketed in multiples of one thousand names. Until you have at least 1000 names in one or another of your mailing list files, you do not have a saleable list.

Names can be sold outright or leased for one-time use. When selling a list, which is *not* a good idea, bundle your cards in multiples of 1000. They can be sold to any mailing list broker. The price you receive will depend somewhat on market conditions, the particular product or service you sell, and on whether your list contains purchasers or inquirers who did not buy.

Leasing of names for a mailing list usually will run from $15 to $50 or more for one-time use. Thus, you can lease your mailing list many times over, turning these names into additional profits for you.

To get customers for your lists, you will either have to advertise its availability or work through a list broker. This additional advertising is not recommended, primarily because of its cost, so long as list leasing is not your main business. In working through a broker you will receive only a percentage of his charge for leasing your list, but he is likely to find many more customers for it than you could. After all, his only business is mailing lists and he can be considered an expert in the subject. When your list is large enough, and recent enough to be considered fairly clean, contact several list brokers and discuss arrangements with them.

To find a broker, check the yellow pages of the telephone directory for any large city under "Mailing Lists." There may be brokers in your city as well. You may also wish to join the Direct Mail/Marketing Association, 6 East 43rd Street, New York, NY 10017, and subscribe to their magazine, *Reporter of Direct Mail Advertising* or read it in your public library.

There is information of much interest to mail order dealers in this magazine and a number of mailing list brokers advertise in its columns in every issue.

When you lease your list to another company you provide him with only a one-time use, charging the current rate per 1000 names for the type and quality of your list. You *do not* allow the list customer to see your names as this would, in effect, be selling them to him rather cheaply. Instead, he will contract with you for you to mail *his* advertising to the names on your list. You may loan him your cards, however, if he signs a statement that he will not copy your list. To make certain of this, insert one or two cards containing the names and addresses of friends who will inform you should they receive a *second* mailing from your list customer. Receipt of such a second mailing is proof that your list was copied. The contract must specify that the list customer pays the postage on all pieces and pays you the agreed rate for the use of your list. If you are to do the mailing, you will prepare address labels from the cards in your list file, affix these labels to your list customer's mail, and take the mail to the post office.

By the time your card files expand sufficiently to provide you with enough names that you can lease your list, you will probably have at least one person working for you. Your employees can handle the preparation of the labels and the mailing of your list customer's mailing while you tend to the daily routine of your major business effort.

Since there is no limit to the number of times you can lease your mailing list to other companies, it can eventually be a substantial source of supplementary income for you. In fact, there may be times when you are using your list to prepare mailings for several other companies simultaneously.

ADDRESS LABELS FOR MAILING LISTS

When you first begin to use or lease your mailing list, you will be working on a relatively small scale, with perhaps one to two thousand names. Names and addresses can be typed directly on perforated sheets of gummed labels using carbon paper to produce five or more copies at the same time. As you gain more list customers, the names and addresses can be typed on either a paper offset master or on a mimeograph stencil and printed directly on perforated, gummed labels. Remember to use the special offset typewriter ribbon when typing offset masters; and always clean your typewriter type before cutting mimeograph stencils.

There are 33 separate mailing labels to each 8½" x 11" perforated sheet. This requires 31 offset masters or mimeograph stencils for each 1000 names. Mimeograph stencils and paper offset masters are packaged by the quire (25 pieces). Four quires (100 pieces) will be needed for 3000 names.

Mimeograph will be the cheapest method and is perfectly adequate for this purpose. But an advantage paper offset masters have, which is not shared by mimeograph stencils for mailing lists, is that additional offset masters can be printed before printing address label sheets. These duplicate masters can later be used to print more labels, eliminating the tedious job of retyping to cut more mimeograph stencils.

CLEANING YOUR MAILING LISTS

The value of your mailing lists to the company which leases them is in their accuracy. In other words, the names on your lists must be of persons who actually live at the addresses on your lists. People die, get married and change their names, move away, go into military service, etc. This means that as time passes some of the names on your lists become dead names, persons no longer reachable at the addresses given. Mail to dead names is wasted and the money it cost for materials, preparation, and postage is completely lost. If you do nothing to keep the names on your lists alive, they will soon become worthless to you as a source of income.

Printing "Address Correction Requested" on your envelopes used for mailings to customers helps, but to really make sure your mailing list is up-to-date, it should be cleaned periodically. Cleaning a mailing list means checking that each name and address in each list represents an actual person and location. This must be done periodically, usually once or twice a year, depending upon the amount of use a list gets. Cleaning costs money, probably much more than you are willing to spend, but it can also earn money because recently cleaned lists lease for higher rates than those cleaned some time ago.

Address verification cards provided by the post office are used to clean a list. The cost to you for address verification cards will be $1 per name, or $1000 per 1000 names, and results are guaranteed by the U.S. Postal Service. An address label is attached to the card, postage is paid, and your return address added. These cards reach the post office in the town to which they are addressed and employees of the postal service check each name and address, noting whether it is currently valid, and return the cards to you. They do not provide a forwarding address if any of your addressees have moved but merely indicate that they are dead names.

With these cards it is a simple matter to go through your mailing list files and remove the cards containing dead names. They must also be removed from any existing offset masters and printed address labels. Draw a diagonal line with a reproducible pencil across each dead name on each master. Do the same on each sheet of printed labels, using an ordinary pen or pencil. Labels so canceled are discarded when label sheets are separated to prepare a mailing.

Remember that you must lease your list many times merely to pay the cost of a single cleaning. If you do not have enough list lease customers to make cleaning practical, you may decide to lease the list during its first year and then sell it. This must be a personal decision and depends almost entirely upon the volume of list leasing business you can obtain on a continuing basis.

FINDING THE OPTIMUM SELLING PRICE

The price you are charging for your product may not be the price which will result in the greatest profits for you. It may be too high or it may be too low. Sometimes increasing your price will bring in approximately the same number of orders but more real income, and in some cases the number of orders will actually increase. In other situations, lowering your price will increase the number of orders so that your income and profits will be greater. Although there is no way to determine the optimum selling price ahead of time, you can test different prices over a period of time to determine the price you should charge.

Assume that you have a product which you are certain a large number of people will buy. At what price should it be sold to bring you the greatest profits? You can determine this with reasonable accuracy in a simple test by offering it at different prices to different groups of people.

First, determine what the nearest similar product now available in stores or by mail order is selling for. Suppose this is $4.98, a typical price at retail for an item costing 87¢ at the manufacturer/wholesaler level. You can probably make a fair profit if you sell it for $3 and possibly even less. However, you want the *maximum profit* possible. It is impossible to foresee the effects of price differences but they will show up during the test.

Have order slips printed, all identical *except for the price,* with the same item being offered at $3, $4, $5, and $6. As inquiries come in, an equal number of persons should be offered your product at different prices. Actually, you should mail perhaps 250 mailing pieces at each of the four prices, thus testing on 1000 inquiries. Keep a close record of the number of orders received at each price *and the gross profit total of orders at each price*. The price which delivers the highest gross profit is the optimum selling price for your product. It is the selling price which *puts the largest number of dollars in your pocket*.

To quickly determine gross profit for each selling price, multiply the cost per order (from the income vs. advertising chart shown in figure 10-3) by the number of orders received at one selling price (a). Then multiply that number of orders by the cost to you of each item sold (b). Add these two products together (c). Then subtract this sum (c) from the total number of dollars received for items sold at one price (d). The resulting figures in dollars is your gross profit after advertising and inventory costs are deducted. This figure will be largest for the optimum selling price. The method of calculating gross profit per each price to determine optimum selling price is detailed below.

(a) Advertising cost = Cost per order x Number of orders received at that selling price
(b) Inventory cost = Cost per item x Number of items sold at that selling price
(c) Advertising cost
  + Inventory cost

  _____

  = Sales cost
(d) Number of dollars received at that selling price
  − Sales cost

  _____

  = Gross profit for that selling price

In some cases you may find almost identical gross profit figures resulting from two different selling prices. Establish your offer at the higher selling price and monitor results. Should your profits diminish, revert to the lower selling price which originally resulted in substantially the same gross profits.

Remember, it's the profits that count, not just the sales volume. If you earn more profit selling fewer items at a higher price than you earn at a lower price, even if sales volume rises at the lower price, stay with whatever brings you the greatest *profits*. And if the lowest price brings the greatest profits, the lower price is the key to success. Strive always to make your *profits* as large as possible.

MONEY-CONSERVING HINTS

Do not use your checking account to hold excess funds which are not needed in the conduct of your business in the near future. Very few checking accounts pay interest and idle money should be put to work. It belongs in a savings account but *not* in the bank which handles your checking account.

Savings and loan associations and savings societies consistently pay higher rates of interest than commercial banks and savings and loan associations in California, Alaska, and Nevada pay higher interest rates on savings than associations in other states pay. Most of these pay interest from day of deposit to day of withdrawal, with interest compounded daily and credited quarterly. Such accounts earn the most money on your excess funds.

Each account is insured to $40,000. By all means, invest your excess funds in a savings and loan association, preferably in one of the three highest-paying states. All deposits and withdrawals are handled by mail and usually the savings and loan association pays the postage both ways. Withdrawals may be made at any time, usually taking less than a week from withdrawal request to receipt of a check.

Suppliers generally offer a small discount on invoices if paid within a specific period, usually 10 to 30 days from receipt. This prompt payment discount can range to 2 to 3 percent and occasionally higher. Even if it is only a fraction of 1 percent, it is still a saving of money. Always pay bills promptly if a discount is offered. Otherwise pay the net amount within the usual 30 days allowed.

If you deal in a product, you can generally save money by ordering in larger quantities. Price breakdowns usually occur at quantities of approximately 10, 100, 250, 500, 1000, 2500, 5000, and 10,000 units. For example, you can purchase 1000 units at a lower cost per item than 500 or 950, and at a lower cost total than for 999. Always purchase the largest quantities you can feel certain of selling each time you order.

When purchasing in large quantities, it is not usually necessary to accept delivery all at one time. Most suppliers will stagger shipments to you at intervals you specify, in effect providing free storage for you and reducing the amount of space you need for your inventory. This also assures you of always receiving fresh merchandise.

Your printer can help save you money. Consider his suggestions regarding printing methods, copy composition, and choice of paper weight, surface, and quality. Use the least costly methods which will produce acceptable results. A large part of your overhead expenses are represented by printing costs. Savings in this area can be important over a period of time. Your printer will also offer lower per-unit prices for larger printing runs. Take advantage of these quantity prices if you are reasonably sure you will be able to use the additional material effectively.

Careful attention to the wording of your classified ads to reduce the number of words and lines of type while still retaining a hard-hitting message will reduce advertising costs. Savings can be used to place ads in additional periodicals, reaching more potential customers and increasing your profits.

Most periodicals offer a lower price per insertion if you contract to place your ad a specified number of times each year. Since you will be running your ad several times a year in each periodical you use, take advantage of this savings and contract for the number of insertions which suit your advertising campaign.

You may eventually decide to place all your ads through an advertising agency. While this service costs you nothing, it doesn't save anything but a small amount of money in postage. However, it can save you time which you can use to advantage in other phases of the operation of your business.

Other money-saving ideas, which can really add up, include leasing or selling your files of names and addresses, as discussed in chapter 12, and keeping accurate records of all business expenses. Business expenses are deductible in full as legitimate costs of doing business and will keep your income taxes at the legal minimum.

You can expand your business operation with tie-in products and/or services and use your files to inform old customers of your new products from time to time. When advantageous to do so, place additional classified ads to attract more readers to your new tie-ins.

Optimize your selling price structure as soon as possible after starting in business to maximize your profits. Aim for the highest possible income after expenses have been deducted. Methods of doing this are discussed earlier in this chapter.

DROP SHIPMENTS

Drop shipping is the foundation upon which many successful mail order businesses have been built. What it means is that the products you sell are shipped directly to your customers by the manufacturers or wholesalers. You never handle them.

Advantages of Drop Shipping
Drop shipping offers so many advantages that it should be considered before any final decision is made regarding the products to be sold or the type of business you decide to start. Some of the main advantages are:

1. You need invest no capital in stock.
2. You need no storage facilities for stock.
3. You do not need to pack and ship merchandise.
4. You can usually obtain all or most of your follow-up sales materials from your suppliers at much lower costs than your printer could charge.
5. Sales materials provided by your suppliers are professionally prepared and often include photographs and color.
6. Your customers pay you your profits and pay for the merchandise you sell before you order it from your supplier.
7. You need very little space or equipment to operate a drop ship business. A desk, chair, file cards, typewriter, and shipping labels are all you need to start.

8. You can start in operation with only enough capital to pay for a classified ad and the mailing of your follow-up advertising to your potential customers.
9. Within a very short time your business will be operating on money supplied entirely by your customers.

Although the advantages in favor of drop shipping are of great importance, there are also some disadvantages which you should consider carefully before making a final decision. Perhaps the most important disadvantage is that a number of other mail order companies also have drop ship arrangements with the same suppliers. Another is that retail prices are often established by the supplier and already printed in the sales literature he provides. This can limit your profits, and since others are selling exactly the same merchandise at the same prices your market is diluted. These major disadvantages apply *only* if you arrange a drop ship agreement with a single supplier and offer only his products to your customers.

The best way to reap the benefits of drop shipping and minimize its adverse effects is simply to make drop ship arrangements with several suppliers. Offer your customers several products of each supplier. You should probably not use the supplier's catalogs but should develop your own sales literature. However, if sales aids in the form of slips, inserts, folders, leaflets, etc., are available from the supplier, you should use these if they describe the products you wish to sell. If only a complete catalog is available, use it as an information source to develop your own sales literature. In this way you do not compete directly with any other drop ship mail order company. Instead, you offer a unique selection of merchandise which your customers can order directly from you.

How Drop Shipping Works

Those persons who reply to your classified ads are mailed sales literature describing all the different products you wish to offer. When an order arrives it will be accompanied by payment in full at the retail price or your established selling price. This payment includes not only the amount you must forward to your suppliers (the wholesale price) *but also your profit*. You receive your profit *before* you pay for ordered merchandise—and *you pay for merchandise with the customer's money*, not your own.

To process an order, you separate the merchandise ordered by the customer into groups to be drop shipped by each different supplier. You then type the customer's name and address on one of your own shipping labels, typing as many labels as suppliers whose products are listed on the customer's order.

You then prepare your own order to each supplier, listing the merchandise to be shipped to each customer, inserting the wholesale price. Orders and labels are then mailed to each supplier with payment for the wholesale cost of the merchandise. Your work is finished—except for depositing your profit into your bank account. The difference between the amount of money the customer sent you and the wholesale cost of the merchandise is all gross profit for you.

When the supplier receives your order and labels he fills each order, packing and wrapping it, pastes your label on the package, adds postage, and mails it directly to your customer. Your check for the wholesale price of the merchandise is deposited by the supplier. The customer receives his order promptly and usually will be well satisfied. Drop ship suppliers are businessmen, and to succeed they must handle orders rapidly and maintain the quality of their merchandise. You seldom need worry on this account. Most drop ship suppliers depend wholly upon small mail order companies like yours for their business. They want you to succeed, because the more you sell the more money they will earn.

Very rarely will drop shipped merchandise be returned to you for refund in compliance with your guarantee. Refund the customer's money promptly.

You should, if possible, arrange with your suppliers to return unwanted merchandise to them for credit. In most cases they will agree to this. You merely forego your profit on the merchandise returned, plus the cost of shipment back to the supplier.

Control of a drop ship operation and the filing system you need are exactly the same as explained in preceding chapters. The only difference is that you do not personally handle the actual merchandise. Your files and their functions are exactly the same as if you purchased the merchandise for resale and shipped it to your customers yourself.

Glossary

ACRONYM—An artificial or coined word formed from the initial letters of a phrase.

ADVERTISING AGENCY—A business which functions as intermediary between client and media, capable of doing professional market and product research, testing, preparation and placement of all types of advertising in various media.

AGATE LINE—A line of type such as commonly seen in newspaper classifieds, and used for billing purposes. Sets approximately 14 lines of type per inch.

AGATE TYPE—Type of 5½ points per em. Commonly used in classified advertisements and normally set solid.

AGENCY COMMISSION—Payment made by newspapers and magazines to advertising agencies when advertising is placed by that agency. Normally 15 percent of the normal space charge for the advertisement.

ARO—After Receipt of Order. Usually used on quotations to indicate delivery will be made at some specific time after an order has been received.

ART BOARD—Heavy cardboard with one surface pure white (usually). Used for artwork and the construction of mechanicals.

BASIS WEIGHT—A measure of the heaviness of a paper. It varies with the class of paper considered.

BLANKET—A resilient material, usually rubber, which accepts ink from a printing plate and transfers it to paper. Part of an offset printing press.

BODY COPY—Text of an ad, sales literature, etc., as opposed to headlines or display type.

BOLDFACE—A typeface with characters that are heavier than the same style of regular type.

BRISTOL BOARD—See ART BOARD.

BROADSIDE—A printed sheet normally the size of a newspaper page used to carry sales messages.

BROCHURE—A large leaflet or small pamphlet, usually without a cover. Can be quite elaborate.

BUDGET—On business records, a particular expense category to which a specific payment is charged.

BULK MAIL—Third class mail which consists wholly of advertising or similar material, mailable by permit at a reduced rate in minimum quantities of 200 pieces, or by the pound.

BULLETS—Round, solid dots used to set off lists or separate phrases in print. Measured by diameter in points.

BURNING IN—The process by which an offset plate is exposed to light through a negative.

BURNISH—To rub down the surface of a mechanical so all elements are flat and firmly in place.

BUSINESS REPLY MAIL—Mail for which payment of postage by the addressee is guaranteed. It requires a permit. Cards and envelopes printed with the appropriate wording and permit number are sent to prospects to make it easy for them to send in an order.

CALENDERED—Descriptive of a smooth, shiny, slick surface on paper.

CAMERA READY—Complete artwork or mechanical ready to be photographed for eventual plate-making and printing.

CARD STOCK—Cardboard or very thick paper.

CLEANING—The process of testing a mailing list to eliminate names and addresses not currently valid.

COLD COMPOSITION—Preparation of copy by typewriter or photocomposing machine, as opposed to setting type in metal.

COLUMN INCH—Space one inch high and the width of one column. Used to describe the amount of space in a display advertisement. Unit of space charged for by print media for display ads.

CONDENSED TYPE—Typeface with letters narrower than normal for that particular face.

COPY—Text. See BODY COPY.

COPY BLOCK—A block of text. See BODY COPY.

COPY CAMERA—A camera used primarily for photographing artwork and mechanicals. It produces a negative on film or paper.

COPY ELEMENTS—Copy blocks, display heads, artwork, etc., all a part of a mechanical.

COPYRIGHT—Legal notice of ownership of certain rights in a published work.

CROP MARKS—Short lines outside the reproducible area of artwork or mechanical indicating margins of the area to be reproduced.

CUT—An engraving of artwork or photograph intended to be reproduced by letterpress. See also PHOTOENGRAVING.

CUT LINE—Line of small type placed immediately below and adjacent to a printed artwork crediting its source or copyright owner.

DEADLINE—Date by which some action must be completed. Used to express the latest date for receipt of an advertisement to appear in a specific future issue of a periodical.

DEAD NAMES—Names on a mailing list of persons who are no longer in residence at the address given.

DIE-CUT—Perforated or irregularly shaped paper or card stock.

DIRECT MAIL—The mailing of advertisements and sales messages directly to potential customers, either blind or upon request.

DISCOUNT—A rebate or lower price offered for payment within a specified time or for buying a specified quantity or dollar volume per order.

DISPLAY TYPE—Large type used as headlines or to attract attention.

DROP SHIP—The process whereby a supplier will ship his products in your name to your customers upon receipt of instructions and payment from you.

ELITE—A standard typewriter typeface producing 12 letters per inch.

EM—A square whose dimensions in points are identical with a particular type size.

ENGRAVING—See CUT; PHOTOENGRAVING.

ENTREPRENEUR—Any person who starts and operates a business.

ENVELOPE STUFFERS—Mailing pieces to be inserted in an envelope and mailed to existing or potential customers.

EOM—End Of Month. Normally used on invoices and quotations to indicate when payment is desired.

EXPANDED TYPE—A type with wider than normal letters for the specific typeface. See also CONDENSED TYPE.

FINAL SIZE—The size that material will be when printed and trimmed.

FIRST CLASS MAIL—The fastest and most expensive method of mailing within the United States.

FOB—Free On Board. Used to indicate the point at which the shipping costs cease to be the responsibility of the shipper and become the responsibility of the buyer.

FOLDER—A small, folded mailing piece.

FOLLOW-UP ADVERTISING—The sales pieces sent to each person replying to an advertisement and intended to induce the inquirer to place an order.

GLOSSY—A photograph with a smooth, slick, shiny surface.

GOTHIC TYPE—A family of typefaces without tails or finishing strokes on letters. See also SANS SERIF.

GRAPHIC ARTS—All the operations comprising designing, composing, and reproducing printed matter.

GROSS INCOME—The total amount of income from all sources during a specified period. See also NET INCOME.

GROSS PROFIT—The total income derived from sales during a specified period. See also NET PROFIT.

HALFTONE—A piece of art such as a photograph which is broken up by a screen and printed as a series of dots.

HARD COPY—Any material which is camera ready. See CAMERA READY.

HEAD—Headline or heading, usually in larger type than the copy it introduces. See DISPLAY TYPE.

HOT METAL—A method of typesetting in which molten metal is forced into a matrix to form letters. See LINOTYPE and MONOTYPE.

IMPRESSION—A single hit of the press, producing a printed sheet.

INSERT—Any single slip of paper containing advertising which is included in a mailing to a potential customer.

INSERTION—The appearance of an advertisement in any one issue of any periodical.

INVOICE—A form used in business to present a bill.

JOB PRINTER—Any small, local printing business.

JUSTIFIED—Describes copy that is set so both margins are even. Type may also be set with the one margin justified and the other margin "ragged," as is the type normally produced by a typewriter.

KEY—A code identifying advertisements so the resultant inquiries may be credited to the periodical responsible.

LAYOUT—The overall design of printed material or artwork. Can be roughly sketched or finished neatly.

LAZY WORDS—In advertising, any words which do not actively aid in getting the sales message across to the reader.

LEADING—Extra space between lines of type, usually measured in points, which increases legibility.

LEAFLET—A form of mailing piece similar to a folder but usually printed on paper rather than card stock.

LETTERPRESS—A method of printing using raised type which is inked and directly applied to paper to produce printed materials.

LINE RATE—The price charged by a magazine or newspaper for each line of an ad.

LINOTYPE—A typesetting machine which casts an entire line of type on a single metal slug, using molten metal.

LIST BROKER—A person whose primary occupation is the buying, selling, leasing, and compiling of mailing lists.

LOWERCASE—Alphabet letters which are not capital letters.

MAILING LIST—A list of names and addresses of potential customers to whom sales appeals may be sent by direct mail.

MAILING PIECE—Any piece of sales literature including order blanks and return envelopes mailed to a potential customer.

MARKET RESEARCH—Investigations of the probable acceptance of a product or service by the public conducted by mail or by personal interview.

MASTER—See PLATE.

MATTE—A dull, soft-appearing surface, usually of a photograph, and usually not suited for high-quality reproduction. See GLOSSY.

MECHANICAL—A camera-ready layout ready to be photographed prior to platemaking and printing.

MEDIA—Plural of MEDIUM. Refers to presentation of advertising materials directly to the public. Includes radio, television, newspapers, magazines, handbills, sky writing, posters, bumper stickers, billboards, transportation cards, packaging, etc.

MERCHANDISING—A term covering all aspects of preparing, promoting, and presenting a product or service to potential customers.

METAL PLATE—An offset plate made of a thin sheet of metal, usually aluminum.

MILLINE RATE—A method of comparing the costs of reaching readers in similar media. Equivalent to the line rate x 1,000,000 ÷ circulation. The milline rate does not allow consideration of the quality of the markets.

MONOTYPE—A typesetting machine which casts individual letters in molten metal.

NEGATIVE—A paper or film copy of artwork or mechanical with black and white areas reversed, used to prepare offset plates.

NET INCOME—Total money remaining of gross income after all expenses have been deducted.

NET PROFIT—Total money remaining of gross profit after all associated expenses have been deducted.

NONREPRODUCIBLE—That which does not reproduce. Usually refers to the color or composition of a pencil lead or other marking device which does not register photographically or is unaffected by ink.

NOVELTY ITEM—Anything unusual or unexpected. Usually refers to a "fun product" or to an unusual form of mailing piece.

OFFSET PLATE—The metal or paper master used to print by the offset method.

OFFSET PRINTING—A method of printing wherein the impression from the plate is transferred to a blanket and then to the paper. See also BLANKET.

OFFSET RIBBON—A special typewriter ribbon which allows composition of copy directly on a paper offset plate using an ordinary typewriter.

OPAQUING—The repairing with paint or adhesive film of pinholes, scratches, and other defects in a negative to be used in platemaking for offset printing.

OPTIMUM PRICE—The selling price which produces the highest net profit.

ORDER SPIKE—A sharpened wire or spike mounted through a weighted base. Used to impale paper for temporary storage of bills, receipts, notes, and other papers.

OVERHEAD—All expenditures incurred as a direct result of doing business; business expenses (such as rent, utilities, depreciation, printing costs). Does not include personal expenses.

OVERLAY—A protective covering over artwork or a mechanical. May be plastic or paper and may or may not contain markings intended for eventual printing.

OVERSIZE—Larger than final size. Usually applied to artwork or mechanicals which are intended to be photographically reduced before printing. See also FINAL SIZE.

PAMPHLET—A small booklet.

PAPER PLATE—An offset master made of paper with a specially treated surface.

PERIODICAL—Any newspaper or magazine published on a scheduled basis.

PHOTOCOMPOSITION—See COLD COMPOSITION.

PHOTOENGRAVING—The process by which a cut for letterpress is made. Artwork is photographed and the negative is used to expose a thick metal sheet. The metal is then treated chemically and immersed in an etching bath. The etched sheet is attached to a hardwood block, becoming a cut or photoengraving for reproduction by letterpress.

PHOTO OFFSET PREPARATION—The process of producing an offset plate from original artwork or mechanical by a photographic process.

PICA—Twelve points or $1/6$ inch. The measure of an em of 12-point type. Also the name of a standard typewriter typeface which produces 10 characters to the inch.

PICA EM—An em of 12-point type. A square 12 points on each side.

PICA RULE—A ruler or straightedge calibrated in inches, picas, and points: sometimes also calibrated in agate lines.

PLATE—A paper, plastic, or metal sheet used for offset printing. Areas to be printed are treated to accept ink, while areas not to be printed repel ink.

POINT—A measurement of type equal to $1/72$ of an inch or $1/12$ pica. Twelve-points are equivalent to $1/6$ inch.

POSTAGE METER—An office machine which prints prepaid postage notices on gummed tape or directly on envelopes.

POSTAGE SCALE—An accurate scale for weighing mail so correct postage may be determined. Calibrated in ounces and fractions to a maximum of one or two pounds. Some automatically indicate postage amounts for different classes of mail.

PRODUCT RESEARCH—Similar to market research, but includes the search for a suitable product to match the needs of an existing market. See also MARKET RESEARCH.

PROOF (REPRO PROOF)—A carefully reproduced piece of copy, art, or display type on heavy, smooth paper. Normally used to prepare displays, artwork, and mechanicals.

PROOF PRESS—A manually operated press normally used only to pull proofs of copy composed in metal.

PROOFREADING—The process of comparing typeset material with the copy from which it was composed so errors may be eliminated before printing.

PUBLICATION—Same as a periodical, but includes other printed material intended for distribution or sale such as books and pamphlets not always published on a repetitive schedule. See also PERIODICAL.

PURCHASE ORDER—An order from buyer to seller authorizing shipment of goods listed thereon. A printed form used by most commercial businesses to control all purchases.

QUOTATION—A statement by the seller of his willingness to sell a specified quantity of an item at a stipulated price for a limited period of time. See also RFQ.

RAG CONTENT—A specified amount of fiber, usually cotton or flax, used in making paper.

RAGGED—"Unjustified"; refers to lines of type in a copy block that are of uneven lengths at one or both ends. See JUSTIFIED.

REAM—A measure of paper quantity; 500 sheets.

REDUCTION—The process of producing a film negative that has a smaller image area than that of the original artwork or mechanical. Specified as a percentage of one linear dimension to which the original is to be reduced.

REPRODUCIBLE—Anything capable of being reproduced in print. Applied usually to marking devices, photographic prints, and other artwork.

RFQ—Request For Quotation. A printed form used to request a seller to quote his selling price for described items in specified quantities.

ROMAN—A family of typefaces identified by serifs (tails at the ends of each letter).

SANS SERIF—Descriptive of a typeface without tails or finishing strokes at the ends of letters. See GOTHIC.

SCREEN—A sheet of glass or plastic with its surface covered with a fine grid. Used when photographing tone art such as photographs, wash drawings, or oil paintings to produce a screened negative to be used in plate-making.

SCRIPT—A family of typefaces which appear as stylized handwriting.

SECOND CHANCE OFFER—A mailing of advertising materials to a potential customer who did not order when he was given the initial opportunity.

SELF-MAILER—A mailing piece designed so that it may be sent through the mails without being enclosed in an envelope.

SERIF—A tail or small finishing stroke decorating letters of the alphabet. Descriptive of Roman typefaces. See ROMAN.

SHADING—The artistic modification of a line drawing which gives it the appearance of depth, solidity, and perspective.

SLIP—Single sheet of paper of a size for insertion into an envelope without folding, usually printed with a sales message or coupon.

SLUG—A cast metal bar containing a single line of type. See LINOTYPE; vs. MONOTYPE.

SOLID—Describes lines of type set as close together as possible with no extra leading.

STRIPPING—Covering an error in copy with a correction on a separate piece of paper. Adding one negative to another by taping it to a clear window in the second negative.

SUBHEAD—A subordinate headline.

SULPHITE—A paper made entirely of wood fibers.

TESTIMONIAL—A written communication praising a product, service, or operation, usually in the form of a letter from a satisfied customer.

THIRD CLASS MAIL—A class of mail for printed matter and merchandise not heavy enough for parcel post. It is less expensive than first class mail and is widely used to mail advertising materials to potential customers.

TICKLER—A file set up by days of the month or week to control the flow of necessary papers within a filing system.

TIE-IN—A product or service similar to a main product and marketed in association with it.

TRIM SIZE—Final size. Usually refers to a bound booklet or pad which is actually trimmed (cut) to a specified size after printing and binding.

UPPERCASE—Capital letters. Opposite of lowercase.

WHITE SPACE—Actual space, regardless of color, between printed copy blocks, artwork, etc. in a layout or in print.

X-ACTO KNIFE—A brand name of a pencil-shaped knife with disposable blades, widely used in graphic arts.

ZIP-A-TONE—One brand of adhesive-backed plastic film used in the preparation of artwork and mechanicals.

Index